LOVE, SEX AND INDIA

The
Agents f Ishq
Anthology

Edited by
Paromita Vohra

cntxt

First published by Context, an imprint of Westland Books, a division of Nasadiya Technologies Private Limited, in 2025

No. 269/2B, First Floor, 'Irai Arul', Vimalraj Street, Nethaji Nagar, Allappakkam Main Road, Maduravoyal, Chennai 600095

Westland, the Westland logo, Context and the Context logo are the trademarks of Nasadiya Technologies Private Limited, or its affiliates.

Anthology copyright © Parodevi Pictures
Selection and introduction © Paromita Vohra 2025

Copyright for the individual contributions vests with the respective rights holders.

ISBN: 9789371971317

10 9 8 7 6 5 4 3 2 1

The views and opinions expressed in this work are the authors' own and the facts are as reported by them, and the publisher is in no way liable for the same.

All rights reserved

Typeset by Jojy Philip

Printed at Parksons Graphics Pvt. Ltd

No part of this book may be reproduced, or stored in a retrieval system, or transmitted in any form or by any means, electronic, mechanical, photocopying, recording, or otherwise, without express written permission of the publisher.

LOVE, SEX AND INDIA

PAROMITA VOHRA is a filmmaker and writer whose body of truth-telling, playful and intensely sensuous work spans documentary films, music videos, art installations, television programming, screenplays and writing of all kinds. Her films include the landmark *UnLimited Girls* and *Q2P*. She is the writer of the film *Khamosh Pani*, several comics, the play *Ishqiya Dharavi Ishtyle* and a weekly newspaper column, *ParoNormal Activity*, which she wrote for fifteen years. She has also written an agony aunty column at several points in her career. In 2015 she founded Agents of Ishq, now India's best-loved digital platform about love, sex and desire. Her antakshari skills are legendary, according to her.

Contents

Foreword: Because Sex Is the Education   ix
Paromita Vohra

At First it Seemed …

Ayye! The Rebellion I Staged to Save My   3
'Dirty' Sidney Sheldons
Deepti Sreeram

The Women Who Bathed Together   11
Arya Jayan

My Period Turns Me On in Ways You Can't   16
Imagine (As Told to a Lover)
Shubha

Uncle's Fault   19
Anika Eliz Baby

I Took a Nude Selfie. It Changed My Life   25
Sruthi Krishnan

Savita Bhabhi and I: A True Love Story   32
Sumit Kumar

The Adorable Boys Who Love 'Papa Bear'   38
Ankur Mehta

Farmati Hoon   47
Meher Bhagat

Where It Breathes   48
Hansa Thapliyal

The Romance of Friendship

I Have Erotic Friendships and It's Not Complicated *Aditya Vikram Shrivastava*	51
My Mother's Lost Friendships *Runi*	59
You Are My Di! *Praveena Shivram*	65
Love Was a Stereotype. Friendship was Radical. And Then, I Met Her *Namrata Mukherjee*	72
Body and Other Requirements for Sex *Aditi Ghatole*	86

Undoing the World

Diary of an Indian Sex Educator *Srinidhi Raghavan*	91
Unfuckable Me *Aliza Khan*	97
Of Simps, Sluts and My Time in a Boys' Club *Nayana Vaccharajani*	104
Why Men Don't Talk About Masturbators—and Other Questions You Never Thought to Ask *Abhishek Anicca*	110
As a Man, am I Condemned to Choose Violence Over Love? Maybe Not *Pawan Hans Badwal*	114
From Lost and Found Poems of a Girl Who Liked Sex *Nisha Susan*	123

A Place in Between

I Believe in the Promises Made by Passing Strangers: Cruising and the City *Anindya Shankar Das*	127
More Than an Identity: How I Realised My Struggle was with Being Sexual, Not Homosexual *Debasmita Das*	139

Main Apni Sabse Favourite Hoon: Chronicles of an Instaspam Queen *Sneha Annavarapu*	146
My Struggle To Live and Love With Vaginismus *Tara*	153
The Prostitute and the Saviour *Arina Alam*	161
I Came Out to My Mom and Now I Think She's Fomosexual *Sharvari Sastry*	165
Travel With Me *Kiran Kakade*	171

Sex Actually

Encounters Women Can't Forget	175
My First Time Taught Me How Not to Have Sex *Jasmin*	177
The Chap Who Would Have Made a Good App *Chitra*	181
Sex Is Something Nice Two People Do When They Love Each Other *Rita K.*	183
Firefighting *Ubon*	188
A Kind of Boring One-Night Stand *Anonymous*	189
Is This Love That I'm Feeling (In My Loins)? *Anonymous*	193
Raw Onions and the Moon *Brishti*	194
Liberated By Sex, Unexpectedly *Jennifer*	195
Intimate from the Get-Go! *Karmasutra*	196

Compartmentalised *Lisa*	198
Letting Go of a 'Great Guy' *Ahenbla*	199
The Ghost of Aziz Ansari *Yo Tambien*	200
The Woman in the Closet *Anshumaan Sathe*	203

Yearning, Searching, Finding

I Dreamt of Having a Suhaag Raat Straight Out of the Movie *Kama Sutra*. My Actual Experience was Nothing Like It *Rimli Bhattacharya*	217
We Met on Grindr. Now the Intimacy of the Sex We Had Makes It Hard For Me to Forget Him *Complex Character*	221
This Is Who I Am: How I Found Myself in Kink *Kevin*	228
Jeep Mein Beep, Dil Mein Dhak *Kavita Devi Bundelkhandi*	236
Hyenas, Orangutans and Discovering My (A)Sexuality *Lonav Ojha*	241
My Male Friends and I Talked About Sex Constantly, But Not How We Really Felt About It *Sudhamshu Mitra*	247
Happy Ending *Pragya Lal*	256
Acknowledgements	258

Foreword

Because Sex Is the Education

PAROMITA VOHRA

I would like to introduce you to this kaleidoscopic collection about intimacy and pleasure, love and heartbreak, sex and beauty, experiments and mistakes, this book of personal stories, with a personal story of my own. It takes emotional courage really—this act of asking someone to listen to your story. I've always found it hard. It requires you to be vulnerable—fragile as a hibiscus, nakedly waiting for the tender attentiveness the world so regularly denies us.

The stories in this book, the ten years of receiving them at Agents of Ishq and editing them, co-shaping them, have helped me to tentatively reach for this courage. So, I court here your indulgence and the beauty of your listening heart. Okay? Okay.

In 2008, I was asked to write a story for an anthology of Indian contemporary erotica. I agreed in a grinning spirit of play because it was edited by my friend. I had never written an erotic story before. But I had read enough and had strong opinions on them, and this, as we know, is enough for the young and the opinionated.

One of these opinions was that some stories seemed to be written as if once removed, with self-conscious stylisation.

They seemed more interested in signalling something—sophistication perhaps?—than turning anyone on. As if they wanted to say they were liberated enough to talk about sexuality but not so crude as to talk about sex itself. Then there were others, written with robust intent to arouse and to afford sensual pleasure alongside literary pleasure. I wasn't confused about which I preferred. So I jumped in to write something that would, at the risk of failure, as in any seduction, turn people on.

In short, the story had plenty of explicit sex in an unlikely fantasy plot featuring time travel and numerous intimacies with a much-desired and barely disguised (well, he was naked for most of the story) movie star.

To be honest, rather than modest, most people reacted to the story with delight. Numerous positive reviews followed. A few stern responses also arrived, and they intrigued me. 'It reads like porn written for men, not erotica written for women,' said one man, who identified himself as progressive. 'You are a feminist and an intellectual. How can you write such trash?' said a woman friend, almost in pain. One gent was upset that there were mostly descriptions of the man's body, but not the woman's. Pointing out that the story was written in the first person from a woman's point of view caused his distress to double. 'Yes, why write in the first person, it makes us think it is you!' One post-colonial writer type I ran into said—before we even exchanged any hellos—'So, I hear you have become a purveyor of porn!' And he was only quarter-joking. A gleeful fantasy had caused some discomfort to the progressive.

So many assumptions coursed below these remarks. The division of porn for men and erotica for women; the idea that not only do men and women want two distinct things but also that those things are the same for all men and women—a default state of gendered preferences. Other genders do not even feature in this imagination. There were pronouncements about taste. A story so committed to revelling in sex and popular pleasures was coarse, even trashy, and, by extension, so was the woman who had written it. A more oblique narrative, more metaphorical, perhaps, delicate as a handkerchief edged with lace, preferably devoted to social issues, would be more acceptable. Taste was not personal here, but a judgement, a veiled censoriousness.

I have often wondered why these reactions, even if they pricked for a moment, never unleashed shame or self-doubt in me. What made me able to trust the responses of those who loved the story while feeling amused by the censorious ones? What enabled me to take away the understanding that while we often imagine that censorious voices are the norm when it comes to sexual matters, they may (as with this story) in fact be the minority, and not represent how the majority feel about sex—or life itself?

It is not, dear readers, because I grew up in a sex-positive commune. But it does have something to do with how I grew up.

Like any other middle-class Indian kid, I had no sex education in school and devoted considerable time to developing pseudo-scientific theories of how babies got into tummies. In later life, I had my own share of posturing and shame around my desires, like anyone else. But I understood only after many conversations with many people that there was one fortunate difference. In my home, sensory delight was an everyday thing, not fetishised or overstated—just enjoyed. Poring over shade cards with excitement, when the car had to be painted (we chose Capricorn green, because that was my sun sign). The smells of an ever-growing repertoire of borrowed recipes filled us with anticipation long before it was time to eat. To memorise poems, to play cards and music, to lose oneself in a book or in singing a song was considered natural and necessary. Naughty jokes we did not understand were in the air, as grown-ups twinkled at each other, time with friends was encouraged and hugs were plentifully shared. We were best friends with our senses.

I would be forty years old before I understood how generous this legacy was, despite the hurts and complications of families that were also my particular lot. Pleasure was not rationed in my home, and now I understand that this gave me, an otherwise awkward misfit, a confidence in the knowledge of my senses. It was this that enabled me, through the adversities and discouragements that social structures, institutions and frenemies throw our way, to do the hardest of things—believe in what I liked, rather than be governed by what others disliked. This small thing was like a rope in a turbulent river that I clung to and which helped me know myself and slowly, if painfully, accept myself outside their expectations and judgement. And it was how, most of all, I learnt over time not to hide from my desires—whether sexual, romantic or artistic—to always confess them to myself even if I hadn't the confidence to admit them to others. I'm not saying it was easy, just that it was infinitely possible.

So, it's hardly surprising that I responded to many things in the world by creating a project like Agents of Ishq, which the stories in this book made their home. That is how it happened—it was not us judging if they were worth it; instead, they chose us. The writers decided that their stories were worth telling, but only on Agents of Ishq. And this is how that came to be.

Agents of Ishq was created in 2014. It was conceived as an art project about sex, love and desire which would experiment with the medium of the internet to create honest conversations about sex, love and desire for Indians, free from binaries. These were not only binaries of gender (male and female, man and woman) or sexuality (straight and queer) but also those of progressive and regressive, modern and traditional, love and sex, good and bad. All the things that keep the conversation on sex segmented and controlled, proxy for segmented and controlling our very selves. It was for this reason that only one word was explicitly forbidden on Agents of Ishq—that lofty whip-like word, 'problematic'. I imagined AOI as a universe of beauty, fun, sensuality and learning. Sexual health, silly quizzes, popular culture, ancient eroticism, emotional questions, naughty poems, histories of sexual ideas would hold hands to create an inclusive and ever-widening frame in an undefined conversation about desire.

We wanted to transform the limited interpretation of sex as penetrative intercourse and relationships as only those recognised by mapping all the registers of intimate life. Here, sex, love, crushes, infatuation, yearning, fucking, dating, erotica, love poems and poems about masturbation, social histories and explainers about consent, queerness and law would all exist on the same plane, neither one more or less important than the other in a real-world, experiential language of sex and intimacy. Monogamy, polyamory, friendship, uncategorisable emotional connections, long-distance love, self-love, asexuality—none of these would be positioned as superior to others. The website was in Hinglish. We used sometimes beautiful original art, sometimes Bollywood images, sometimes ancient miniatures. Double meanings were plentiful, and lust was seen with the same earnestness as intellectual inquiry.

Everything in Agents of Ishq, even the 'List of Sexually Transmitted Infections' and the 'Right Contraceptive Match for You', was cocooned in an atmosphere of pleasure and fun, quite distant from the air of censoriousness and euphemism that surrounds intimate life everywhere else. We would not breathe the air of inhibition! The project would be a garden under the sea, a landscape in the sky—sparkling with mischief, smiling with pleasure, thinking without judging, stating without asserting. In it, each thing that titillates the senses—touch, images, movement, beauty, fun, music, poetry, puns, dance, theory—must be present, the rarefied and the common, both in one place, allowing an affectionate inclusion.

By refusing to be pigeonholed, by keeping all definitions open and in play, I believed we could evolve a new shape. And we would do it along with others—what it is today fashionable to term co-creation, but what in those days we just called idealism. The ones who had never had sex, the ones who saw themselves as sexual connoisseurs and all the others in between would equally shape the contours of this conversation.

We had no impact plan, no defined outcome. Just a hope that the gesture of invitation would determine the nature of the response. Only poetry can say what I hoped would happen which was, as e.e. cummings wrote:

> your slightest look easily will unclose me
> though i have closed myself as fingers,
> you open always petal by petal myself as Spring opens
> (touching skillfully, mysteriously) her first rose

We wanted to be that slightest look of love, not the scrutinising gaze.

Or maybe only a Bollywood song can express what we wanted to suggest: 'Aao huzoor tumko, sitaraon mein le chaloon/Dil jhoom jaaye aisi, baharon mein le chaloon.' (Give me your grace, so I can take you to the stars/Take you to a place, whose sights will make your heart dance).

We wanted to be partners in a romantic adventure.

Clearly, both a poem and a pop song can express our desires. As is the case with our desire, it's not an either/or. Could it happen? Will they, won't they? Well, in one of those starlit moments of beauty, it did.

In the first week of launching the website, we were flooded with emails, many of which had the subject line: 'I too want to be an Agent of Ishq/How can I be an Agent of Ishq?' And just like that, it seemed an entire universe of Indian sexual life opened up, one that had been obscured by a limited (and limiting) mainstream gaze.

Each one interpreted what it was to be an Agent of Ishq differently. Some sent art, some sent poems. And unexpectedly, some began sending us narratives about their own sexual lives.

The stories people sent us fit into none of the templates that the sex surveys and assertions about Indian sexuality impose on us. Sometimes, they did not even feature sex. They were about first times, kisses, marriage, friendship, heartbreak, family, romance and sex of all kinds. They were different interpretations of what makes up our intimate lives. In story after story, what unfolded was a world throbbing with sensory awareness, an appetite for pleasure, which revealed a beauty, self-awareness, vulnerability, sexual strength and, most of all, a deep insight into life. Even stories about traumatic experiences held a tensile self-possession; a desire to determine the meaning of their wound and the terms of its healing.

When invited with no hint of shame and without the pressure to present their narrative in a narrow political frame, people offered stories of great openness, full of layers and contradictions, without pontification and false moralities— either progressive or regressive. It was a dazzling array of voices and experience, and a dozen languages entering the English, giving it new lilts—all the better to telling stories true to their contexts.

AK, a young man of twenty-one, wrote of a first kiss: 'He smooched me, and it felt like some unusual, sweet taste entered from his mouth into mine; a taste my lips would never be able to let go of.' He did not feel the slightest need to preface his tale with, 'I am gay.' He took it for granted and expected it of us as well.

'As for the erection? When addressed to one who it desires, and one who desires it, it is simply paradise on Earth. It should be photographed, drawn, filmed, written, sung, sculpted … Why do we never see it?' wrote Elise, a painter of male nudes, in a rare account of a woman gazing upon men.

'I was building a reputation as That Queer Person, as That Queer Artist and, among my friends, as That Relentlessly Gay Friend. In truth, just as a person, I had no clue how to navigate my love and sex life,' wrote twenty-two-year-old Debasmita about a journey not limited to coming out.

Satya, nineteen, yearned for a girl who is scared of sex and satisfied himself with drinking her in: 'Her eyes are adorable. She wears glasses. I drown in her eyes. Her hair has a peculiar perfume which I just love. She wears only one earring. She's a bit odd but I really like her so very much.'

'I remember writing in my schoolmate's autograph book, "I LOVE: talking to you on the phone" and "I HATE: friendship with boys," recounted thirty-eight-year-old Sripriya, making us laugh at how most of us have had a phase of puritanism.

'All our childhood theories (built carefully by our elders) about how babies are made, like "babies are sent by gods" and "sitting too close to boys will make you pregnant" were shattered in a minute. The revelations were worse than learning that Milind Soman has gotten married!' was one hilarious response to a sex education class, revealing that sex-ed is not just about information.

'I was thirty-eight. Most of my other relationships had ended within two months. So, I never ever got to say, "I have a boyfriend,"' went one achingly honest essay.

'To my, "Dude, where's your condom?" he gave a sheepish grin and admitted he hadn't brought any. Classic. I had some condoms on me though (I always do!), and retrieved them from my purse, only to see him frowning. Long story short, he refused to put one on,' wrote one person about adventures in dating, an early mention of what we now know as 'stealthing'.

Sometimes, the writing astonished us with its beauty and lucidity. Sometimes, the writing was not polished, the feelings muddled. But if making documentary films has taught me one thing, it is how to listen acutely and ask the question that leads to deeper understanding. From each narrative, working with the writer, we drew out the experience together, made the writing clearer without trying to erase the regional inflections in the syntax.

Sometimes, this took six days. Other times, it took six months. We were chasing no deadlines or numbers. We wanted to shape these narratives as journeys, not clickbait. We did not want to call them 'crowdsourced'. We were building a new sexual and emotional conversation together.

The more stories we shared, the more people sent their stories. We never mandated topics, we never invited anything specific. There was no syllabus. The readers decided what was relevant to the topic of sexual life, and the readers revealed new ways of sense-making that reshaped our understanding—including all of us in the AOI team.

Through the stories of sex, love, desire, people shared, really, a part of themselves. These stories revealed ever new ideas of what is considered sexual, what it means to be Indian, what it means to be Indian *and* sexual.

Sex, romance, love, desire, being horny, being lovesick, choosing celibacy, self-pleasure and mutual pleasure are, glory be, not a matching dinner set from which we eat with tasteful propriety. It's a potluck, a rambunctious banquet, a feast that those who fast may also smilingly attend.

In the decade since Agents of Ishq began, a lot has changed. Sexuality influencers are the new 'It' folks. Their evangelism and education are to be celebrated in one way. But there is that sneaky feeling that so much instruction is undergirded by homogenisation. For a long time, we spoke about sex mostly in terms of violence, disease or sexism. We spoke of sex as politics, sex as culture, even sex as aspiration. We spoke of the attitude to sex—to signal we are liberated and set ourselves apart from those we called prudish. As the market has increasingly colonised the world of desire and sex and love, we may even speak of the aptitude for sex—how many positions have you tried, how to give a blow job, how to achieve an orgasm in five ways.

Social media drowns out our own thoughts with constant judgements on red flags and 'problematic' things. We are encouraged to share our stories, but with identical language, its meaning mandated through terminology and jargon. Sexuality education becomes a kind of evangelism, which schools the swirling galaxy of desire, disciplines our sensory and emotional intuitions, rather than seeing them as a place that births knowledge, poetry and wisdom. In recent years, we have noticed these strictures creeping into submissions, policing their own experiences with jargon. All these conversations around sex often feel like a ruse for not really discussing desire, for not allowing a language to express the nature of intimate life, which is contradictory, unpredictable, unslottable and heterogenous. Something may seem playful to one person and manipulative to another. While experiences may be connected, they are rarely identical. The new sex positivity dictated by social media all too often replaces old norms with new ones because it strips experiences of context and of the human truth that resides in granular details.

In this world of neo-conformity, stories remain the most human and so, the most radical thing. The stories of others give our feelings a place to belong. Our experiences may not match, but they give us confidence to think about our own experiences as meaningful. Those are the non-negotiable terms of liberation—to know ourselves and craft our journeys in tandem with others. To love ourselves but also others and so not be lonely.

These stories are quietly radical, for one reason—they refuse to be categorised, taxonomised, classified. They do not conform to some pre-decided framework of permissible experiences. They are heterogenous, they believe in themselves. The single and the attached, the passionate and the detached, all staked a claim on reframing our view of sexuality, rooted in their lived wisdom.

In sharing our experiences, we create a kind of commons, a poetic cloister, in which we may reflect on our own lives and deepen our relationship with ourselves. If these stories have taught me anything, it is that sex itself is the education.

This book is a selection from the deep archive of contemporary Indian sexual life on Agents of Ishq, suggestive of what exists in the world. It doesn't matter who gets what award for sexual education. The people who have shared their stories, these bonafide agents of ishq, are the true vanguard. They give us and each other courage to break the deadlock of anxiety within ourselves, the misconception that if we do not fit in, we cannot belong. These stories have kept a beautiful corner of the Internet alive and unruly—resisting algorithms and hashtags, with always room for one more wildflower, one more story that will change the way we think, change the way we are.

AT FIRST IT SEEMED ...

Ayye! The Rebellion I Staged to Save My 'Dirty' Sidney Sheldons

Amma shamed me in front of my crush, and so I had to have my revenge publicly too!

DEEPTI SREERAM

8 January 2024

I was twelve when I planned my first rebellion, against Amma, who had confiscated my school library books, ripped off the cover of my copy of a Sidney Sheldon novel and screamed into my ears: 'Ayye! Is this why you wake up early? To read dirty books?'

At home, dirt was what my father's feet carried in when he came home after work. As a construction site supervisor who faced the drilling machine every day, Papa collected dust and compliments in his hair and ears. The engineers and the site managers were envious of how relentless my father was. He could finish work caked in dust and smile in the heat knowing that he has saved one more real estate developer from falling behind his deadline.

But when my father returned home, the dust mixed with water and his poor attempts at being clean was *azhukku* for Amma. When azhukku found its way into the corners of the sofa, the nooks of my sheets and finally to the ends of my mother's searching broom, Amma would yell a guttural *ayye!* Her throat would convulse in the scream, and in her haste to sweep off the dirt, she would bang the walls with the broomstick as if everything needed a quick beating. Years later, I would learn that my mother borrowed this cry from her beloved friend Lakshmi Subramanian, who refused to cross our gates, for fear that the beach smell and poor hygiene would give her an *ookanam*. At the end of the story, Amma would say that the gag reflex was a reminder to not be 'azhukku pennugal' (dirty women).

So, when my Amma screamed *ayye!* and pushed me off the stoop I was reading on, I was seething inside. If I had to hold someone responsible for bringing dirty books into my life, I would have dragged my Chechi by the hair. It was on my sister's bed that I discovered the first bound copy of Sidney Sheldon, wrapped in her old pink churidar, hidden from my mother's razor-sharp eyes.

That afternoon, when I discovered the book under my sister's embroidered white pillow, I traced my hand through the bold lettering of the title, *Tell Me Your Dreams,* and wondered how pretty Sidney was. Was she blonde like the woman on the cover? Did she write a book to defeat her sister's pettiness? At that age when I started reading the Sheldons and the Steels, I had firmly believed that Danielle Steel was a man and Sheldon a woman. Only women's heads could produce pages of thrill that would make you sit upright and devour books. If Amma could make six *puttus* in one hour along with chickpea curry and run off to catch a bus to her school, women could do everything.

But, an hour later, I was cursing Sidney and her ancestors, ruing the day my sister tricked me into reading this dirty book with dirtier words. With my insides stuck to my panties and my stomach cradling a stone, I walked towards the bedroom my parents slept in. 'Is this how you made me?' I murmured. 'You dirty monsters.'

Tell Me Your Dreams had all the smells of a thriller. A lonely woman fleeing from the gaze of an unknown stalker. The Nancy Drews I'd read had a quieter start where she kissed Ned, chilled out with her girls and discovered a mystery.

Until that moment, before I had run to the bed and found Sheldon, I had a reliable and chaste woman narrator in my head who kissed (perhaps?) and solved a mystery. When the book ended, she would eat scones or drive her Mustang into the sunset. But Sheldon's Ashley Patterson? Ashley was unreliable, scared and sexually charged. Every kiss with Ashley was a full-blown tongue-to-tongue atrocity where men would 'dip' into her mouth and mix saliva. And then, just when I was making sense of the French kiss, words like 'tumescent penis' would stick to me, reminding me of the day I dipped my hand into the sticky gooey atta that Amma made only to shriek at the stubborn *mavu* that went into my fingernails. *Take it off, Take it off,* I had screamed.

In *The Getaway Car,* Ann Patchett says she found her first adult novel, *Humboldt's Gift,* at fifteen. Although she admits to not understanding much of the book, Patchett says with certainty that she still remembers the imagery and emotion to this day. But how to live with the image that sex involves the dirty job of mashing one *susu*-producing organ with another? Everyone says your first is special. Amma said first children like my sister are special. But what if the first book that introduced me to sex was also a first book of French kisses, incest, castration, blowjobs? How to feel the *romancham* that erotica promises when the first experience of fantasy is soaked in dirt?

Remember, I was twelve. It had only been a few months since that biology class when Naina Miss left us with 'the sperm and the ova meet to create the zygote' and asked us to quickly flip the page to sexually transmitted diseases without solving the original question: how does the sperm meet the ova? After a year and a half of beating my head over this, I had thought that I knew the answer when I saw Mohanlal and Urvashi disappear into a bedroom for their first night on TV.

'The sperm flies into the air, meets the ova and becomes the baby!' I declared to my gang of girls. The declaration was followed by a detailed demonstration where I taught biology to the entire class far better than Naina Miss. At the end of it, even with the rapid Q&A, I had scored a spectacular win among friends.

'But what about the *vayaru* squeezing? Why do they play with the belly button?'

'It is the hole for the sperm to enter.'

'Why do they drink milk?'

'Do you expect birthing a baby to be an easy process? Milk is necessary.'

I still remember that day with fondness. The sight of Nimisha looking up to me. The squeezes on my arm for solving the mystery that had haunted us night after night. Even when Anjitha, the eternal *samshayam rogi*, suggested the physical insertion of the male urinary organ as the way forward, I had asked her to urgently revisit her understanding of hygiene.

It is not that I was a good girl before Sheldon. By six, I had written my first love letter to the silver-toothed Robin and asked him to kiss me during PT period. At eleven, another love letter to a boy called Ranjith. But these fantasies were so clean that Amma would have said *nalla vrithiyulla manassu* (very clean mind) if she saw the white rooms adorned with white curtains, where I loved Roby or Ranjith, under the scent of Lizol and Surf.

Even when the other girls carried napkins into bathrooms, I was the sentry at the doors covering them from surveying boys. When they learnt to sit with blood, I revelled in the protection that I offered to the girls in class. In this flat-chest, no-periods phase, I was flying through corridors, jumping over short boys, throwing my dupatta and climbing over *perayka* trees to catch red ants that attacked Nimisha. So, what will Patchett say when a fantasy breaks and the dirt of your first imagery seeps in?

But the body responds fast. This I learnt after I took membership to the local library to find more Sheldons. After knowing that my insides felt a strange, gooey feeling when Ashley had sex, I knew that I had always wanted a bit of that *azhukku* feeling. Yes, the mavu dough that stuck to my fingernails was awful but then addictive the minute I dipped into the dough, kneaded it with my fists and pressed it into shapes—how did I miss the sensuousness of it? How did I forget the love I gave to the cake batter bowl when I licked the traces of chocolate off carefully with my tongue?

My story after this is like the fizz that pours out of the Coca Cola bottle. Whenever the week ended, I would hurry to the Sanmargadarshini library (ironically translated to 'the library that shows the virtuous path') to find a Sheldon and get dirty. Sometimes, dirty thoughts would leak into my schoolwork and make me destroy notebooks. Other times, they would find their way into my head when I saw my crush Moinuddhin walking towards me.

All of this felt good until Amma yelled *ayye!* at me in front of Moinuddhin, who had come to borrow my maths notes. In her shriek, I sensed her friend Lakshmi's disgust, Amma's shame and Moinuddhin's embarrassment at seeing me squirm. The secret joy of reading Sheldon and fantasising about Moinuddhin was now mixed with many unbearable historic layers of humiliations that my mother gifted.

I had not thought of revenge against Amma until I noticed how she shied away from saying sex out loud. Once, when Amma was narrating the story of a movie, which had a rape scene, she said, 'And then ... something bad happened.' Whenever Amma said that, Chechi and I would ask about what had happened, again and again. But she would never say what it was. She would never explain why she did not let us watch the song in *Devaraagam* where a moaning Sridevi lay in the grass while a perspiring Arvind Swamy watched from above.

Yet I have seen her share covert glances with Papa when they remembered their letter-writing days. At their first meeting, Papa had fallen for Amma when she had come in with a sari that was threatening to fall off her waist. 'Your Amma had the flattest stomach,' my father said with a guffaw when we asked why they married each other. But these conversations were a minute long and punctuated by throats being cleared. When Amma once proceeded to explain how Papa had written a five-page letter when they were newly married, there was a further frenzy of throat clearing and a quick teasing back-and-forth that did not divulge any information. 'Your Papa is a romantic man,' she said, and with that, Amma had ended the conversation with a smile and a nod.

Even Papa who had happily given us a teaser to their romantic times, had a *kalla* (shifty) look when we sat before the TV. Once, when the channel stopped at the song 'Kehdona, kehdona, you are my Soniya', Papa saw Kareena Kapoor's strap threatening to fall off from her shoulder while she was dancing with Hrithik. When I made a pointed remark on the strap's flimsiness, my father dove for the remote and changed the channel to Asianet News.

My plan was to stage a similar if not bigger humiliation where Amma would get a collective *ayye!* from everyone around. So, on the day our uncles arrived from the Gulf, when my father was seated at the table eating *meen* curry, I asked: 'Amma, you married Papa in 1981 but you had Chechi in 1985. Why did you and Papa have no babies for four years?'

Like any good detective, I had noticed how my mother could not take unexpected questions before a public audience. Quizzing her on sex inside the kitchen would lead to a careful answer where she would say, '*Daivam thannila*' (gods did not bless us) or '*Athinoke athintethaya samayam und*' (there is always a time for this).

But before my uncles, Amma and Papa were caught off guard.

'Well ... that is ...' started Papa.

'You could not have kids,' I said to Amma.

'No, that is not it,' Papa muttered, with emphasis on 'it'.

'You did not want kids,' offered the uncles.

'No, no,' Amma said, glancing quickly at them.

'You did not ...'

'No, stop. We, I mean we ... Papa was in the Gulf no, soon after marriage. And he came on leave after four years ...'

As my mother's voice trailed off, the room had gone quiet. My uncles were now eating rice ferociously while my father was looking at the staircase with purpose.

'So, Papa came in 1985 and Chechi was born, and then he came in 1987, I was born ...'

'Kunji,' my father began cautioning me as soon as he realised the ball was dropping.

'*Ayye!* So you are saying that Papa and you had sex during summer vacay—' the last of what I wanted to say drowned under my sister's fingers and my uncles' collective throat clearing. When I looked up, Amma had her hand on her throat.

Days later, when I woke up, the Sheldon was back on my shelf with better binding and a tiny inscription from my mother: *Don't read this when you have exams.*

Deepti is an aspiring writer and a surviving PhD student.

The Women Who Bathed Together

Arya, for the first time, glimpses her aunt's breasts and wishes to never have boobs

ARYA JAYAN

28 November 2022

The first breasts I ever saw were my aunt's. We were bathing in the pond and walking out of the water to soap ourselves. She carefully undraped the *mundu* that she was wearing to tie it tighter before she could go for her swim. I looked at my flat chest and wondered about things I still could not decipher.

I still believe Amma got married to Achcha to enjoy swimming in the ponds surrounding my grandmother's place. Hers was a small house isolated from the world but surrounded by mango trees and three ponds. No wonder my grandfather moved there after marriage. And, when all his three sons were married off to wives who loved swimming, the women followed a tradition—they would all go for a swim together, laugh and play in the water, and then leave with red eyes for the temple to pray.

The green pond used to scare me. When I was at an age where Amma bathed me, I would accompany these women, including my Chechi—who was six years older than me—and watch them bathe. The gushing of the water and the occasional slithering of a water snake scared me. I would dip my feet in the green water and watch the fishes snuffle at my feet. But I envied Chechi, my older sister. She could dive in from one end and pop up at another, water streaming down her face.

And then there was A. A and I grew up together, she was just a month younger than me. She was the prodigal daughter of the family, the one everyone wanted me to be. She would sit beside me to watch the TV and all I wanted to do was push her into the pond. I always found her to be the annoying sibling but I still loved her. We both did, in spaces where we did not exist together.

One summer, when Amma and Achcha left me in Kerala for their sanity, my mischievous aunt decided to torture me. She pulled me onto her lap, massaged my hair with oil and carried me to the pond. There, she dropped me into the water as she removed her clothes. I thrashed around, struggling to stand even though it was summer and the water was shallow.

She yelled, 'Aryu, just beat your legs and you'll be fine!' I somehow did beat my legs hard enough to be able to float, but the pain of water lodged in my nostrils made me give up. My aunt lovingly took me in her arms and caressed my face until I came back to life. This did not stop me from joining these daily baths.

Summer mornings are the best time to immerse yourself in the water. A and I would strip ourselves naked and plunge into the water. She would swim around in circles while I dove to tickle her underwater. Chechi would be washing her clothes next to my aunt. My aunt told A and I that Chechi was a big girl now and she needed to wash her own clothes. Chechi couldn't strip herself naked, she would wrap herself in a white towel before she went for her swim. I wondered why, until it hit me: just like my aunt, Chechi also had grown breasts.

I remember that one instance when Amma called Chechi to her room and locked the door. Amma held out a packet with a half-naked lady on it and asked her to start wearing the new thing. Chechi would complain about feeling suffocated, as if plastic hands were constricting her chest. I never quite understood why until one day when I saw her mundu fall. My aunt told her to tie that thing even tighter. At that point, I realised I did not want boobs at all. I just wanted to swim free without the mundu.

Chechi would dip into the pool slowly, swim around and leave. Then it was just my aunt and us. As we grew older, my aunt would talk to us more. She would recite O.N.V. Kurupu's poems or even play antakshari with my sister as we bathed. Once, she joined us for the bath, dove to the bed and found a rock shaped like a chapati. She held it between two fingers and flung it across the surface of the water. The rock skipped five times and plopped back below. I thought she was a magician but soon she taught us to skip stones. Chechi, A and I would collect rocks before going for a bath so we could skip them across. Once, I threw a stone right into A's eye!

The pond was never quiet. When we would leave after our bath, the water snake would emerge for its swim, its head gliding above the surface. The turtle would trundle up the shore to eat the moss and kingfishers would dive to grab fishes that once ate my feet. It was their home that we women enjoyed the most.

As summers grew hotter, the pond grew smaller. Once, before my aunt could splash the water to make its residents aware that we were visiting, the water snake crept its way around the pond. It wasn't scared. It was swimming in circles and would stop and look at us women. What a pervy snake! The snake always had to greet us. It would wait for the women to oil their hair and walk towards the steps of the pond. As we removed our clothes, it would stick its head out. In my mind, our naked bodies excited it and its tongue would slither out of its mouth. It kept doing so whenever we showed up.

A month later, the pond was cleaned and the snake was taken somewhere else. By then, I was growing in places I hadn't really thought of before. I could no longer dip my naked body into the water, and my aunt gave me my first mundu.

She tore a piece from her husband's red mundu and wrapped it around my body. She would tuck the end at the top so it stayed, but after two minutes of jumping and swimming, the mundu reached the shore. She would tie it again and it would glide off my body and wander off into the pond. She insisted on it being tied. But I always felt like the mundu never belonged to my body. It was covering me in places I never thought needed to be covered.

The mundu was always considered to be the rite of passage for every woman in my family. But I never wanted my breasts to be held by my uncle's old mundu. It slipped away from my body the second I dove into the pond. It took away the power my legs had as I beat them to swim. Regardless, I was never allowed to be naked anymore.

It seemed as if women were scared to be naked around each other. Perhaps it was difficult to accept that breasts are more than just instruments that convert blood to milk, or cleavage that men stare at from angles unknown. I loved that my body was growing in places. My chest jiggled and my bum had more roundness, but the mundu never allowed me to embrace the wetness of it. And the pond became a distant place every time I bled.

Every time my periods started, I was shunned from the household, no longer a woman or a family member. These practices made me hate being a woman so much that I never understood how beautiful the experience of being one truly is.

Until, one day, when I was on the second day of my period and wanted the comfort of the water over my stomach. When my aunt was away, I dove into the pond naked and felt every pulsating whoosh of the water. It gushed over all parts of my body that were aching and I immediately felt all sorts of sensations. When the old blood tissue escaped my vagina, fishes gathered, trying to eat the small bits and pieces that floated around. The pond was my resurrection to womanhood.

I also felt alone. The creatures around the pond made noises of their own, but they weren't like the sounds of other women that echoed in my ears. I felt lonely and unwanted.

We all grew up, grew older. New bathrooms were fitted by the side of the house and the water level rose. The women never went together to the pond. The stones were left unattended next to unwashed chaddis and the pervy snake died a tragic death. Even if we decided to go for a swim, we never went there together.

I stand on the gravel steps looking at the green pond that changes colour every time you scoop the water. I don't have anyone to tie my mundu, so I take the longest one and wrap myself as tightly as possible. I float on my back and watch the blue kingfisher look at my breasts. 'Perverted animals,' I think as I turn my back to swim. The mundu unties itself and tangles around my ankles like weighted anklets. There is no ground for me to hold and I can hear the snake laugh from its hole. I breathe in and breathe out water. In turn, I hear the water breathe into my ears.

The sunlight fades as my head drops further below. The green water is black now but from a distance, I hear, 'Aryu, beat your legs and you'll be fine,' and so I do. I move closer and closer to the sound and reach the surface. I open my watered eyes to no one as I breathe the pond out.

My Period Turns Me On in Ways You Can't Imagine (As Told to a Lover)

It has a deeply ferrous tang, seductive like flowers or the night air, but richer, funkier

SHUBHA

10 April 2023

You like to discover little details about me, no? Here's one. I wash my crotch twice when I'm on my period. I've been doing this for so long that it's automatic now, no thinking required. The lather is always pink the first rinse, and smells a little rotten (yes, of course I sniff it, I'm a sniffer—thought you knew that by now). Anyway, I soap again, and the lather is creamy white the second time around. I rinse it off and get on with the rest of my bath.

And now (lucky you) a bonus detail—for some months, not long ago, something splendid wedged itself between the two rinses. I was lathering vigorously today when the memory of that other short-lived habit rose up through the suds.

I did the first rinse as usual, cleaning away the oxidised maroon gunk from between my thighs. Then I'd take a deep breath and slide a finger into my vagina for some of the fresh stuff, the bright red sauce coating my skin. And then, I'd bring that up to my face for another breath. The deepest breath of all time. The first inhale of the day hits the hardest, the first inhale of the month doubly so. That same briny wallop of a sea breeze, only less salty, rustier, ah, how do I say it—

wait, let me run to the bathroom to sniff at the primary source—no it's too late, my sixth day, only a sour hint of pee now—diving back into memory then—

a deeply ferrous tang, you could call it. Seductive like flowers or the night air, but think richer, funkier—like sweat-drenched silk or too much attar. I'd breathe that in, over and over and over, and it would fill me with a pleasure that is proving visceral to remember but impossible to describe.

Perhaps this would be easier to convey if you were living as I was at that time. Imagine you spend all your time in what can be called a colourless, odourless apartment. You may interact with another human for around sixty seconds this week, and if you do, it'll be with two masks on. All you smell is the freshness of laundry and the dull creaminess of bottled curry paste (in which you cook vegetables that smell of nothing).

The only produce with any bouquet is a bunch of mint. You stuff your face into it, and immediately regret doing that because it hasn't been doubly sanitised and left out to disinfect overnight. This is the sort of spare scentscape in which you stand a heightened chance of observing and appreciating the twang of your own menstrual blood.

It amuses me that I plunged into my vagina for this delight. You know I don't otherwise go there in pursuit of pleasure. My lips have been gloriously sufficient for as long as I can recall, for longer than I've been menstruating, and up until now, my periods were only a dampener when it came to my rich fingering life. If I ever did play around during that time of the month, it was in spite of my period, because a daydream or a conversation with you snowballed into something luscious and irresistible. I would likely pause long enough to spread a towel out below me, and would then run to the sink to wash up afterwards, holding bloody fingers aloft.

But now I find myself here, in this white-tiled bathroom lit with slanted rays of mild spring sunshine, reaching inside time and again for one final whiff of this bottomless ruby glory that presses me up against the wall, that arches my back, that undoes every knot of tension and boredom in my belly. It is a full release and a reliable one, and I find I can plumb its depths for a good deal more. I tell myself to only ride the magic wave, not question it—but of course I will question, because I want this, this pleasure that I have discovered all on my own, that I pursued without anyone telling me that it is something I might or must like. I want it to explain something intrinsic about me.

There surely isn't any virtue involved here, but at least there isn't any murkiness either—a kink for me to treasure, it seems, one so untethered from any sense I have of myself that it comes with no connotation, positive or negative. Someone else may tangle this up with desires to birth, to mother, to nurture, but I know enough of myself to understand that isn't it—the ritual is alive in a way that's all mine. If anything, it conjures visions of a deity—Kali dancing atop the world.

Now, many moons later, I roam the world with a mask stuffed into my back pocket, and my period is once again a minor nuisance instead of a major sensation. I luxuriate instead in the silken salty notes of your skin after a game of badminton, or (sincere apologies for the juxtaposition) in the ripe bouquet of pig's blood before I slurp from my bowl of boat noodles. For now, I lean back, my pleasure taking precedence over the discomfort of the cold, hard tiles, and soak in the scent for a little bit before I start the second rinse.

Uncle's Fault

What I understand now about grooming

ANIKA ELIZ BABY

16 March 2021

An attractive twenty-six-year-old man approaches a sixteen-year-old girl. Sparks fly. That these sparks will later burn her up to her very soul is unknown to the girl. Right then, she only feels joy. She revels in the confidence that she is a mature young lady, attractive enough to win the affection and attention of a mature man.

Ignoring her gut, looking past the nights spent crying and hoping that the man would respond to her texts and treat her better, she will try everything possible to make things work. They had to work. He was the only one who really loved her. After all, he said so himself.

She would carry this heavy weight until college, proudly referring to it as her 'long-distance relationship'. He would cheat first. With another seventeen-year-old girl. Slowly, in the process of discovering herself in college, and not being allowed to break up with him despite wanting to, she would cheat on him too. It was also the only way to get out of an immensely toxic relationship.

'One wrong to set many other wrongs right,' as I would later be told by someone.

The first night, when I told 'uncle' that I had 'cheated' on him, he pulled my hair and held my neck. Uncle slapped himself over and over. We both cried.

On the second night, we sat silently, with me occasionally whimpering 'sorry' between my tears, and him smoking cigarette after cigarette, listing all the places he would have taken me to, and the gifts he would have bought for my upcoming birthday, had I been more sensible. Had I not done this to him.

On the third night, I pointed out to him that he had cheated on me too. He pushed my face aggressively with his finger, and then slapped me ... once, twice, thrice, after which I stopped counting. And that is the story of how I came to hate big rings. The bruises they caused on my face meant I wouldn't be meeting any of my friends the next week. Thankfully, I only had a few friends, because the others had been cut off when my relationship with uncle had begun.

On the fourth night, my apologies would break through. Perhaps the scarred face was an added effect? Or sex was a basic need? Or he believed I had been punished enough to have learnt my lesson? He set me on the table, to undo my dress. He threatened to penetrate me without a condom, just to hear me say no. To listen to my scared and trembling voice, to regain a sense of control over my body, which he had lost the night I had 'cheated'.

Two fingers, one with a big black stone ring, were put in. A declaration was made: it was not tight anymore. I was not a virgin anymore. And, of course, virginity was important for an uncle who wished to marry me. I had not passed his slyly-conducted two-finger test.

It took me a long time to realise that drunk seventeen-year-olds do not cheat, especially if they've never had sex before. It took me more than a year to realise that I had been raped, by yet another older man. I was seventeen and traumatised.

He asked me to pack a sari that day. We were going to an OYO room somewhere far away, because he wanted to run away from his problems. He took me along for comfort and coddling. Another time, a lehenga was the requested attire. He was twenty-eight after all. There were bound to be wedding fantasies. I was his eighteen-year-old *almost*-wife.

An *almost*-wife is like a wife. She performs basic tasks for the *almost*-husband—wash clothes, stitch torn clothes, look pretty. But one must wait for her to become socially appropriate before presenting marriage demands, that is, she must turn *almost* twenty-one or twenty-two.

After a night of one-sided pleasure, I lay on his chest, watching our fingers dance together in the dark. 'Today I overheard some boys from your college. They were talking about you, pairing themselves with you.'

My fingers stopped dancing. 'What? Who? What do you mean, "pairing themselves with me"?'

'I mean they were deciding which one of them would be a good match with you. Saying "you take her", "no, you take her" and all ...'

A young girl, fresh out of high school, in her first year of college, was being traded off—hypothetically—on the tables of a chai shop. I felt vulnerable, insecure. I wanted to disappear into his arms. It was horrible. What was happening?

'What do I do? Do you know who they are?' I whispered into the ears of my wise protector.

'No, but I think from now on you should be careful about how you walk and talk in college. Just don't be so friendly. After all, you are my girl, na?'

A thousand protests erupted in my mind. Why should I change myself? Why should I care? Why was no one shouting at those boys?

But all I whimpered was a sad 'Okay …'

His fingers continued dancing.

How small my hands looked next to his.

⸻

When a much older person establishes contact with a younger person by gaining their trust, usually by taking on the role of a mentor, a boyfriend or a dependable adult, it is called grooming. It is often done to exploit the younger person for sexual pleasure.

Dating an older guy is a kink for many. As a young person figuring out the world, it is very hard to navigate and identify red flags, especially for children from broken homes. I had been groomed by two different men in two different cities. That it happened twice still eats at me. It took me a long time to accept that whatever had happened was not my fault.

Almost two years later, I remain with random memories that catch me unexpectedly on some nasty days, only to choke me and render me completely incapable of functioning.

Every time I think of the way they touched me, I feel dirty, experiencing feelings that make my gut churn … like someone has put a fan, slicing the air above my head, in my stomach.

I remember countless nights of lying in bed, screaming into my pillow until my throat gave out. Jokes didn't seem funny anymore. Blades would inch closer to my skin on cold nights, only to shy away at the last minute. I remember tears alternating with every breath. I remember it all, until the day I froze outside the very same tea shop where I was being—hypothetically—traded. I cannot recollect what happened to me after that moment of freezing. The six months that followed have merged into one big, black blur.

Today, at the slightly more mature age of twenty, as I work to make myself freer, happier, stronger, I want to hold a systemic practice accountable—that deeply embedded aspect of our Indian culture to 'respect elders'.

From a young age, we beat a few terms and conditions down on children—uncle is older, uncle has more experience, uncle knows all, you cannot correct uncle. Children swallow this and begin to depend on any and all uncles who approach them without thinking twice. They don't know that a relationship is meant to be a two-way street, filled with open conversation and mutual respect. Instead, relationships become authoritative. Uncle will tell you something, and you must heed to it, else he will get angry.

Most people don't even realise they are being groomed because of the indoctrination that men, especially older men, know everything, and must not be questioned. We have convinced ourselves that relationships are best only if the man is older than the woman. Grooming is simply the end result of such false 'romantic' ideals. These relationships rely on an imbalance of power.

Groomers have a way of weaselling their way in, promising you that you are 'different' from others. They will convince you that they are not like your parents, but are your 'special' older friend. That the two of you share a unique relationship which your parents cannot comprehend, and so you should not bother to try and share it with them. Before you know it, they are dictating everything you do. You cannot go to certain places, mingle with certain people, because they have done it, they know how 'bad' it is and they are being kind by *looking out for you*.

You are suddenly restricted from important, life-changing experiences. Restricted from becoming an independent, blooming individual with a life of vividly colourful teaching moments. Simply because that does not suit uncle. If you become independent, who will rely on him? What if you become better than him?

Yes, he wants to see you grow, but not grow past the need for him.

If you have found yourself in this situation before, or are in one now, please remember: 'He knows better'? 'He is older'? 'He has more experience'? Okay. Then he should also know better than to mess around with women who are much, much younger than him. Women who are still trying to figure out the world.

It is uncle's fault. It will always be uncle's fault.

At the time of writing, Anika Eliz Baby was a student of St. Joseph's College (Autonomous), Bangalore. When not making memes, she is cracking awkward jokes and fangirling over anybody who is not her. Read more of her writings https://thatswhatbabysaid.home.blog/.

I Took a Nude Selfie.
It Changed My Life

After years of hiding, could a nude selfie get Ini to see her body in a new light?

SRUTHI KRISHNAN

13 July 2020

I grew up in tents.

I wore salwar kameezes that could accommodate a supersize suitcase strapped to me and layered it with dupattas when I was a teenager. If you asked me what colour those billowing wrappers were, I would not be able to tell. If you asked what the texture of the material felt like, were the necks outlined with embroidery, or did the cut resemble a U or V, I would say O. My memories of that time is like a film montage with a me-shaped hole in it. I seem to have taken a magic marker and erased my body painstakingly from every frame. I do not recall my body or my being in it.

How do I explain this absence to you? If you ask me to tell you about my life during those times, I could tell you vivid details of every plot and line I encountered in books, how I tussled with certain words and images, and how certain characters still whisper to me. I can tell you about the libraries. Galaxy, the lending library, was near the railway station. The owner, a tall, dark man, conjured a perfumed halo. A hint of gold peeped out of his shirt. He never spoke much to me. I thought he was one of those Alistair MacLean spies spending time lazing around a book-lined room between missions. I borrowed a book in the morning, finished it on my way to junior college in the bus and, in the evening, rushed to return it to get the next one.

The other library, a *vachanalay*, which signposted a narrow lane, smelt of *agarbattis*. The owner's hair was always oiled; estimates of how many litres of oil were devoted to taming those thick strands makes for fun calculations. He, too, didn't speak much, and let me ponder over the shelves. The silence was not what you would call companionable, but that of benign disinterest. On the other hand, if you ask me about the shape of my hips or my breasts when growing up, I don't know. I never shared a companionable silence with the mirror, and I don't think the disinterest was benign.

I sang. I listened to music. I had the privilege of control over a tape recorder and a ledge by a window where I sat listening to songs late through the night. You couldn't see much outside the window because it had two layers of mesh—one more closely knit to dissuade pigeons and the other a regular *jaali* that seemed to invite more dust than dappled sunlight. At home, I wore nighties, that formless fortress of cloth, made usually of some thick, durable material. The sides were stained with turmeric. After all, why use a towel when your sides had ample reams of cloth too?

The tent was comforting. In a way, as my body lived inside that tent, I didn't need to live inside my body.

I think I was afraid of my body. It felt it was always too much of everything. Others had bodies that seemed tame—they did not insist on peeking between buttons, they obeyed waistbands, they slid into sleeves, they remained cupped in bras and they let bones outline them in sharp relief in photographs. My body seemed like a testament to refusal. My breasts pushed through the sides of bra cups, tugged on straps, my tummy fought with *nadas*, waistbands and button-up jeans, and my arms seemed to resist any sleeve. It felt like constant battle—indented shoulders, branded waists and abraded thighs—every part seemed to rebel against being tied down, stuffed or wrapped. And so, to compromise, I relaxed the sartorial shackles. To be honest, I was afraid I would lose, and my body would take over.

Every shoe I wore would soon develop bestial qualities. Crocodile mouth, I used to call it, for my feet would insist on ripping the seams apart. I remember going to a shoe shop where a bespectacled Gujarati man clad in crinkled pants knelt in front of me, only to laugh at the size of my feet. 'No girl has feet of this size. Go anywhere, you won't find anything that fits,' he declared on behalf of shoe manufacturers worldwide. I looked away, unwilling to meet his eyes or my mother's despairing ones while he turned to my mother's dainty size five feet, hoping she would want to choose a pair from the tempting array displayed all around. He caught me looking hopefully at a particular row and smugly said, 'Those are for gents.'

The world had calibrated, parameterised and standardised who is a girl, and it had been decided by an august committee that I did not fit the specifications. Though I was told I was a girl, shoes made for girls left half my feet unshod; bras struggled to contain spilling flesh; jeans were, well, just not for me. The world screamed, through measurements, labels and laughter, that my body was illegitimate.

But that's just part of the story.

Then, as I was laughing with my friends while exiting a train compartment on the way to a trek, an unknown hand squeezed my left breast. I faltered, confused and turned, not knowing whose face among the hydra that stared back from the train's maw owned that hand. My friends had noticed nothing, and it was as if the fast-receding sensation on my breast was the only tangible moment.

I am not sure how much I want to recount such momentary violations, for there were many. It was as if this body of mine, that was deemed illegitimate, was still fair game in another murky arena. When my dupatta slid away, the eyes of a senior in college immediately darted to my chest, before he looked away, abashed.

Even when I was very young, I understood in an inarticulate way that my body was capable of eliciting desire, but not the wholesome kind that runs cursive in Rose Day cards, smiling in living room photographs, and is given a U certificate. Bodies like mine, it was indicated in several different, deliberate ways, were suited for a different kind of desire—one that was between sheets, either on the bed or in a magazine. In a world spun into a digital web, this other kind of desire was the lifeblood of its most profitable industry, porn. And so, the word best suited to my body was not just illegitimate, it was also illicit.

Many years passed.

I once told a friend who was discussing her boy troubles that they are not something I know too well about. Why, she asked. Well, I began, faltered, and blurted, I'm not pretty, so boys never liked me that way. She stared at me awhile. And said, I think you are confusing 'beautiful' with 'sexy'. We spoke of other things, but over the next few weeks, months, years and decades, her words kept coming back to me. I may not squeeze into the world's mould labelled 'beauty', but did that mean that I was not desirable?

Some more years passed.

Recently, I came across a project called 'Identitty', where an artist, Indu Harikumar, was exploring the relationship women have with their breasts. People shared their stories, and sent a photograph of their breasts to her—and she drew them. She had stopped accepting contributions. But the prompt called out to me—I wanted to write about what I felt about my breasts, and before I knew it, I had typed out a few pages. I sent them to her, thanking her for the project, for it did feel like I had dislodged something within me.

She wrote back, and asked me for a picture. I was petrified. I had just written about that girl who lived in tents, and suddenly, I was back being that girl who tugged on her kameezes, wishing for that tent. I had two choices: I could retreat into that tent, or …

Before I could change my mind, I went to my room, shut the doors and windows, and took my top off. Turning the camera toward me with no clothes on felt like deciding to go buy groceries naked—utterly demented and prosaic at the same time. I remember laughing loudly, almost startling myself.

I could go and read the fourteenth finance commission report and forget all about this escapade. What if someone stole my phone, and made billboards of my boobs. Suppose my phone slipped from my hands while chatting with my mother and in trying to catch the phone, I pressed something and sent the nude to her? It was as if, faced with that unbearable lightness of a selfie, I felt a bit foolish, and that made it all alright. I clicked. Clicked some more.

Some months passed.

I was lying on my bed chatting with someone. I finished the conversation and was just fiddling with the camera. I tried to take a selfie but felt conscious. And then I dipped the camera lower. I unbuttoned. I clicked. This time, I did not think so much.

As I scroll through those images of my naked body, it is as if I am able to gaze upon myself, without looking back at myself, as a mirror is wont to do. I take my time, linger on my folds, the way the skin gleams, the various shades of it. Often, I can't shoot my face with the picture, and so, I become anonymous—I don't know whose body it is. It feels delicious, just watching the skin, the way sometimes body hair curls, and I feel compelled to touch.

Somehow, I was able to distance myself from my own body. It is objectification, of course, but perhaps in being both the person doing the objectification and being objectified, it felt safe. I wondered about how I framed these photographs—was I drawing from a vocabulary that objectified women? Did I want to be seen a certain way? I tried to shoot myself in postures that would usually be deemed unflattering, but even then, watching those photographs, I discovered a new kind of desire, a desire that slowly cut that invisible cord tying it to beauty.

As I walked on roads, I watched people, and thought that naked, all of us have different shapes, desirable shapes. I would like to touch an arm, slide my hand over someone's belly, kiss chubby thighs or stroke bony hips. I sometimes just let my hands glide over my naked body, closing my eyes, and feel skin meet skin, a warmth that speaks of life. It feels like desire, and I do not need to even see myself then. Beauty is about seeing, desire is about touch and want. After bathing, as I dry myself with a towel, I linger here and there, and wonder how the skin of various parts feels so different. I look at pockmarks, darkened patches, stretch marks and gently trace a finger over them, and it just feels like skin.

All these years, I had thought my body was something I had to battle with. And here I was, suddenly wanting to caress myself, massage my legs, bite my own tummy and smell my palm as it wandered over my face.

I met a friend, and I told her about taking these photographs. She wanted to see them. I gave her the phone. She looked at the photos. I watched her face, and something in me unfurled. It was no more my secret; someone else had seen it, seen my body, the one I live in, and we giggled together.

Sruthi lived inside a nightie and read books in an Indian ooru. As the decades passed, all the oorus she had lived in began to clamour for their tales to find a page to sit upon. So, now she burrows into saris, writing books in an Indian ooru.

Savita Bhabhi and I: A True Love Story

*Here is something you should know about me.
I wrote three stories for Savita Bhabhi*

SUMIT KUMAR

4 Mar 2017

Here is something you should know about me. I wrote three stories for *Savita Bhabhi*.

Just three. I wasn't even able to write the porn parts. I am clarifying this not out of fear of the law but out of respect for the creators.

How did I end up writing *Savita Bhabhi* stories?

It started in 2009, when *Savita Bhabhi* had just begun. I was a fresh computer science graduate, freelancing for a magazine. My friend and I were working on our design start-up. And I had just started work on my first graphic novel, which was to be a serious Pakistan–India *dhishkyaun shahkar*.

The first few *Savita Bhabhi* episodes had come out and I, like everyone else, was reading them all. Some ideas are so strong that sometimes their treatment doesn't really matter. I don't mean to say that the concept of Savita Bhabhi was treated badly. The artwork of the first comic—*The Bra Salesman*—is really good. The ones that followed had good artwork too but it was the concept that sparked my engine, and I guess everyone else's as well.

Then I got on the *Savita Bhabhi* forum. This was before you could stream porn online, or at least before I could. Forums were a great place to find good porn. By good porn, I mean, the porn that works for you at that moment in time. I find the stories in porn films to be exceptional. The stories of the good old, full-length porn movies border on the absurd. But between the absurdity and the bad acting, it somehow creates something that is actually not bad—something unusual. Recent porn films, which are shot in HD and want to be tasteful, no longer have that strange quality. It is difficult to explain. I think it's because you get the feeling that the new films take themselves very seriously and the old ones didn't.

Anyway, I thought the *Savita Bhabhi* forum would have gold. Instead, I saw their invitation asking for stories from readers. So, I shared my story idea, which was inspired by the graphic novel I was working on.

I was deep into research then: Tarbela Dam, Afghanistan, behaviour of frontier tribes, etc. So the story I wrote was this: Savita Bhabhi goes to Afghanistan to catch Osama Bin Laden on behalf of the USA. She lures him out of hiding and fucks him till he's tired and ready to surrender.

Why did I feel like writing a story for *Savita Bhabhi*? Well, I like humour and I want to be a part of funny things. I saw *Savita Bhabhi* as something funny, something naughty that I could write. I can craft an absurd plot. It might not be good, but I can write one.

The next day, I got an email from a 'Deshmukh'—the pseudonym for the owner of *Savita Bhabhi*. He liked the story and wanted me to flesh it out, although he suggested we change the location to Shimla and he'd rather have a dacoit instead of Osama. I was cool with it. He asked me to send him a rough plot and that he'd take care of the rest. I did my bit, he did his, and *Savita in Shimla* was out soon.

And then I went out, feeling wonderful, like an invisible Republic Day parade was on. Immediately afterwards, I bumped into my buddy Adhiraj Singh and the staff of what was then *Random* magazine (today, Comic Con India). How I showed off! *Badi santushti mili.* As someone who draws, I liked the illustrations. They were done. I have never been a perfect anatomy, third angle to the fifth perspective, *aur pata nahi kya* guy. I just draw, *theek deekhey toh badhiya.* So I was happy.

A few weeks later, I suggested another idea and Deshmukh responded. This time I was exploring my 'krativity'—Savita won't be at the house, she would be at her *maayka*. Her husband Ashok would be at home, alone. He would be visited by the cablewallah, doodhwallah etc., and none of them charge him. In their flashbacks would be their sequences with Savita Bhabhi. The story would end with Ashok congratulating Savita Bhabhi on her good management of the home.

Here too, Deshmukh edited the storyline and wrote the porn himself. I did write the porn, but he told me, 'Lovemaking isn't alternate *oohs* and *aahs*,' (which is quite true). And I loved my absurd plots more than writing the erotic parts. I have always been in a hurry, and hurry is bad for lovemaking.

So I stuck to what I knew best—providing the storyline.

But I asked him to credit me, that is, to mention my name on the cover. He was unsure, since usually, everyone got pseudonymous credits like FunkY!@bb. I just didn't understand why people wouldn't want their name on something so cool. Or did they not think it was cool? Maybe they were not Indians? Or maybe they were and they knew their *chacha* read it? *Pata nahi.*

But yeah, I got my full credit, and I'll always be proud of it. Nobody in my bloodline can top that.

Deshmukh later asked me to write for a third time for a new comic series he was planning, and this time he (actually, I have never been sure if Deshmukh was he or she) was ready to pay me. They wanted me to sign a contract with some company based in Isle of Man, an island located between England and Ireland. I agreed and wrote the story, though by the time that was wrapped up, I was lost in other things in my life and could never get the money.

Then other things happened.

In 2011, I finished my first graphic novel, *The Itch You Can't Scratch*, and on a whim, the publisher and I decided to mention the following on the blurb: 'After writing for *Savita Bhabhi* ...' This small, impulsive act taught me about sensationalism, journalism, ethics, PR agents, everything.

Since my book received wide coverage and the first article about my book called me the creator of the character Savita Bhabhi, Deshmukh was pissed. I wrote to the reporter but she didn't correct it.

During all this, my parents maintained a safe silence. Maybe they knew, maybe they didn't. My graphic novel was about my life and my family. It was honest about poverty. But my sisters were pissed about the honesty with which I had written about our family. The poverty of a Dalit family, the story of my father's brothers who were consumed by it. As an upper-middle-class family now (thanks to my father and reservations), my sisters try to keep that under wraps. They felt shame in me putting it out like that for the world to read.

My eldest sister told me about her issues with the book before she stopped talking to me altogether for some time. About Savita Bhabhi, well, they never spoke of it. My eldest sister once mentioned it once: '*Aur tu ek to ajeeb ajeeb cheezein kar hi chukka hai, wo kya bhabhi waigarah* …' and then she laughed.

That doesn't mean all my relatives were as easy-going.

One of my mamajis gave me a golden lecture on doing 'these bad things' and how he never thought I was 'that kind of boy', I'd seemed so 'normal'. I had made 'these shameful things public' and I had to succeed a lot in life to wash these sins off—*pata nahi kya kya kaha*.

Looking back, I still feel Savita Bhabhi was a powerful character. Obviously she's hot as hell—what draws me to her is the whole *desipana* in an area where Indians send top traffic to adult websites, but still don't create adult content. Also, her character appeals to the teenage boy in me who used to drool over beautiful older buxom women. I have nothing to say in about the character. There's nothing to learn, man, it's just the whole naughtiness of it. That's it. Why do we have to dissect everything? *Roti khaa ke so jao, yaar.*

I do not want to talk about how the character liberates women, etc. In my head, they don't need anyone or any character to liberate them. They are liberated, they liberate themselves. It's an individual who does things. If a serendipitous thing like an encounter with a fictional character helps it, then great. Dissection is a useless debate, which wastes essential time; we can use that time to take action, useful small acts that begin change. Not *bakar bakar* wherever that is just lines of text. *Lorem ipsum. Lo mujhse bhi likhwa liya duniya ne* paragraph. *Zeher kahan hai?*

A lot of people also might pretend to like *Savita Bhabhi* because it's cool to do so, like watching the movie *Gunda* is cool, a kind of cultural slumming it. But I believe the character was a big success because of its relatability. It invoked this dark fantasy for a hot bhabhi, yet kept it slightly funny, catching on to the tone of *Mastram* (the cheap erotic literature, which also inspired a film). Take the story of Savita giving tuitions—a simple act that occurs everywhere is made naughty, and a scenario that's already in the mind of every teen who goes for tuitions. It's just that someone wrote about it.

I would happily do it again.

Sumit Kumar is a cartoonist and founder of the comics and animation studio Bakarmax. He comes from the Dalit community considered 'untouchable' in the Indian caste system. He has been a contributor to Savita Bhabhi, *which ironically made Indians touch themselves.*

The Adorable Boys Who Love 'Papa Bear'

Who decided that desire is only for the young?

ANKUR MEHTA

21 August 2020

I was struck when he said, 'I'm sorry, you are too young for me.'

I looked at the photograph I had sent him via WhatsApp, after long conversations with him on the gay dating app, Grindr. Me, with my thinning hair and a grey beard; I couldn't possibly look young. But to him, I was. And not in a nice way. He wanted someone wrinkled. Older the better. *How could that be desirable*, I thought. But it was, for this strapping young man in his thirties, a professor in a junior college in Mumbai, with his handlebar moustache and thick wrists. I asked him, 'What is the oldest guy you've had sex with?'

'Eighty-five,' he replied.

I had stumbled upon this desire very recently. Young adult men, not boys, men 'ready to settle down' as they say, who loved older men, sexually, and sought them out actively. A young, rather aristocratic looking man, with broad shoulders and long firm thighs, whom I met in Ghaziabad, said he liked men who looked like his father—big, powerful-looking, with moustaches and a protruding belly. I asked him, 'Isn't that incestuous?' I was trying to be funny. He looked rather disgusted at the suggestion. 'I am just describing what I want. My father is the handsomest man I know.' I felt foolish. Desire existed in an unmoderated domain for him, where analysis was an unwanted voyeur. It's what he wanted. And he would settle for nothing else. I was not big enough for him. I also did not have a beard then. Nor a belly.

We assume what people find attractive. Let me rephrase that: I had always assumed what people find attractive. Youth. Fitness. Light skin. Muscled body. Cute face. Beard. I did find that attractive. Still do. But *others* did not necessarily seek out the same thing. The kind of boys who rejected me in my youth were the ones drawn to me as I grew older—attracted to me not despite my age but because of it. Not all of them. But a substantial number. Those who were clear in their profiles: 'Only seeking matures. Young men below 40 please stay away.' Never ever had I felt more desired. Or amazed.

On porn sites, I had seen videos of young guys having sex with older men. Somewhere, maybe without thinking about it much, I'd classified this as an anomaly—desperate youngsters, hypersexual old men. There was money involved, probably.

It couldn't possibly be part of the spectrum of desire. Everyone should love youth, right? That's what everyone tells us. That's how it should be. Old men prey on young women. Old women prey on young women. Old people prey on young people. Right?

I have always known I'm a gay man. However, I did not get along with young gay men when I was young. They felt I was too serious, too mature for them: an old man trapped in a young body. The dismissal was mutual. I didn't quite enjoy the things that young people seemed to like. I did not enjoy alcohol, partying, loud music, dancing, going shopping or watching movies. My tastes were much too boring for them. But though my tastes were 'mature', that did not mean I found 'matures' desirable. I desired the young body. But young men did not desire my body, young though it was.

Gay friends, I felt, approached me for career advice or emotional counselling. I was the big brother they could lean on. The sensible asexual friend. I had (still have) body image issues and so I felt they judged me as for being too fat, too unshapely, for pretending tight clothes fit me, for choosing trousers with elastic bands. I felt I was being rejected for my body and not just my tastes. I didn't belong with this younger generation. I always felt like an outsider and so I invested my time in my work. I never really dated, especially after one serious affair and heartbreak ('You are too practical, no fun').

I focused on my career, rising up the corporate ladder, earning money and finding sexual pleasure in rent boys. These were eager young men easily available on the Internet or other networks for a small fee. It was very convenient for us. They would come, have sex with me, take the money and go away. No clinginess. No mess. No risk and drama of rejection and hurt. No pain of wanting what you can't have.

With some of these men, I struck friendships. At no point did I assume they desired my body. I was nice to them. If they were nice, like wishing me on festivals, I suspected they wanted more money—which was often the case. For me, their arousal when we were together was part of their youth. I did not like it when they would want to watch porn clips, of women mostly, in order to have sex with me. I did not call such guys back. I did not like those who, after sex, insisted they had girlfriends and that sex with men was just a hobby, a way to pass time. This was a turn-off. I would give them money and ask them to leave. I preferred those who did not talk too much, who performed more and proclaimed less. I did not allow myself to feel that they might find my body attractive.

Regardless of my lack of self-confidence in my private space, I was very happy with my life. A single life—with staff to take care of my housekeeping needs; young men to take care of my sexual needs; friends for my social and emotional needs; another group of friends for my intellectual needs. A neatly compartmentalised life, until one day, during the lockdown, I missed them all, and, tired of webinars and video calls, I started spending more time on Grindr.

I couldn't really meet people because of the social distancing norms for health and safety reasons. So I had to satisfy my desires digitally. This is when I stumbled upon what was, for me, a totally new bower in the garden of sexuality—sexy youths who yearn for the companionship of older men, who desire their 'papa bear'.

I was familiar with twink clubs, straight acting clubs, muscle clubs, sugar daddy clubs, bear clubs and otter clubs. This classification is common and casual, especially in the world of dating apps. People are clear about what they want. There are spaces to cater to men who like older men with lots of hair on their bodies and big stomachs. Men who don't like smooth, young boys and a whole range of choices that is not part of popular media. What surprised me was the number of twinks and muscles who liked bears. They saw the Laughing Buddha and Santa Claus as sexual, desirable, delightful beings.

Here were these young, beautiful men who clearly knew what they wanted. They wanted older men and the range varied. Some preferred men who are wrinkled, bent and stooping on a stick, a movie grandfather. Some preferred them to be fit, muscular uncle types. Many of them wanted moustaches. Some wanted wobbly potbellies and jiggly buttocks. Some wanted chests full of grey hair into whose cushiony comfort they could abandon themselves. Many preferred older men who were 'loose'—which means natural, not sculpted in the gym. Regular older men, with dad bods, or shall I say, Indian dad bods.

My world really changed when I grew a beard. I was always clean-shaven and happy to look cherubic, thinking this would attract other men—a calculation with low returns. But the moment I grew a beard and it turned out to be grey, I was in high demand. It took me by surprise. People complimented me for my looks—women, and men. Something had changed. It was the beard that got me attention on Grindr, more than anything else, especially the fact that it was grey. I was now officially 'papa bear'.

For all the porn talk that is popular on Grindr, I was shaken and taken by the genuine kindness, gentleness and romance that I was showered with by these men who sought matures. They were not simply seeking money. They were not simply seeking a body. It was borderless—no compartments. Friendship. Mentorship. Desire. Support. I felt parental, the word is *vatsalya*, or tenderness, combined with the *shringar* and the *madhurya*, the sexual and the romantic. A tenderness between a young man and an older man. A 'pure feeling', as one of the men said, that few understand or give in to.

The young men I met during the lockdown spent hours chatting with me, discussing their careers, nature, politics. I would ask them, 'Don't you have friends your age?' They did. They played PUBG with them. But that was not enough. They found pleasure in men like me—older men, with beards, with experience.

They were not part of the 'gay scene'; they did not want to go to parties. They did not want to meet younger gay men. They were not interested in queer politics. It bored them. Sometimes younger men hit on them and they would laugh about it.

Some of them were stunningly good-looking. They went to gyms to sculpt their body and could be poster boys in gay clubs. They were aware of the impact they had in the gay world, but they were not interested in that. Youth just did not arouse them. And their gym routine was not to attract old people either. They said they love going to gyms because they liked their bodies and wanted to look attractive.

My insecurities returned. What did they want from me? Surely it could not be my body.

You see Bollywood stars and celebrity creators clinging to their youth, with the hair dyes, the face lifts, the tummy tucks, the keto diets and the Instagram posts, fearing old age, fearing rejection, fearing aloneness. But I was now confronted by the opposite: a paradise I had never known before in my life, a paradise I refused to believe could exist, a paradise where I was desired as I was—mature and plump. For me, it was permission to be myself.

Still, you can't help second-guessing: was there something perverse about it, even if you are dealing with adults? Is it the right thing to do, even if the consenting man is a post-graduate in political science? Then you realise there is mutuality here, between two grown-ups, and what's coming in the way is mixed baggage. Where are these rules on how to be gay coming from? Who said only young people fall in love? And why should they only fall in love with young people? Why do we put our desire in boxes made by other people?

What I love about the boys I've met is how full of life they are. One sends me photographs of his haircuts and enjoys me praising them. Another tells me how he cannot talk to his family and prefers staying away. Another wants me to send him selfies every day, doing ordinary things. Another sends me juvenile jokes, and gets upset if I do not reply instantly. One lives in a slum in Mumbra, another lives in his small village near Kota, one is a salesperson from Kakinada, one is a small businessman in Ajmer. One loves to see me nude, one just wants me to send emojis occasionally. The video chats are short, just a kiss, a smile, a moment of adoration, under bed sheets, or from the bathroom, avoiding the scrutiny of family. I see their innocence sometimes, their fears, the burdens placed on the youth by society. These man-boys, looking to sleep on my chest, and feel safe—which is also an important and beautiful function of intimacy.

I have never been monogamous so I chat with multiple people simultaneously. I clarify that I don't like exclusivity. Some do have a problem with that, but most don't. I don't talk about one to the other. I feel that violates privacy. But they know there are others.

Occasionally, they ask me about my 'partner'. I laugh and change the topic. When they try to make me jealous, of other papa bears in their life, I feel relieved. No pressure of being the only one. I have heard stories of possessive boyfriends, drama and even suicide attempts and bouts of depression. That world of clinginess terrifies me. I have coped with aloneness not by seeking the one but by craving the many who also find solace in many.

I am also in high demand because I'm single. I found this out because most of the older men are married. These married men meet younger men in hotel rooms while travelling, for sex which is shrouded in secrecy and maybe self-hate. They don't want to have conversations. These young men are looking for not just sex but also friendship. They don't want to encroach on the married lives of these older men but, treated as guilty secrets, they feel humiliated, denied, deprived, as if they're waiting in the margins for crumbs.

A delightful young banker I know from Jogeshwari in Mumbai hails from a very affluent north Indian family. He told me he was in a relationship with a solicitor from the age of twenty to twenty-three. It ended when the solicitor's wife and children found out. His other relationship was with a civil servant who was twenty years older. For five years, the gentleman would travel to his city and spend so much time with him that his wife got suspicious. She realised this was not just friendship and forced him to break it off. These were long-term relationships, and he is still in touch with those people. He is in his thirties now, with two relationships under his belt. I asked him if he would ever get married, and he said unhesitatingly that he would. He could not push things away for longer. He has to accept the inevitable. He was not too happy about this, but saw it as the way things are, even as they should be. He didn't see anything wrong with loving an older man and having a deep emotional bond with him while being married. He did not see his sexuality as being any impediment to his married life. He was very comfortable with it. There was no anguish or doubt in his head. Would he let his wife have lovers? I asked. He did not reply. The thought had not occurred to him. And what if his children found out? He blocked me. I guess he loved daddies who indulge, not daddies who interrogate. But some papa bears want their lover boys to be decent, not just dashing.

For me, these last few months have been about discovering that fixed notions of how the gay world is or should be were based on propaganda. There are many worlds out there, hidden, but real and thriving, if we look beyond the shadows.

I have seen men who I once felt were out of my league eagerly welcoming me into their fold, enjoying my body, enjoying my maturity. With them, I feel I am myself, not performing, not pretending, not transacting, just being, taking a moment at a time. Yes, maybe these boys are seeking a father figure. And maybe my own erotic and sensual pleasure is mixed with the desire for loving those children I never had. I am not their father and they are not my children. To classify such attraction as 'incest' or 'fetish' is just another way of invalidating different desires. I just want to enjoy this feeling, without analysis or judgement. Let it be what it is—natural.

Ankur Mehta (name changed) is a planning-to-retire IT consultant who lives mostly in Bengaluru but prefers Mysuru, and is often found on the beaches of Bali.

Farmati Hoon

MEHER BHAGAT

Afternoons grow dark with hidden
Thoughts of you
And I'm singing thinking naked
Thoughts of you
I feel myself shimmer, grow sticker with
Thoughts of you
Then I scatter like stars crying out,
Thoughts of you

A poem submitted to the Agents of Ishq annual Masturbation Shayari Contest. Meher Bhagat is a pseudonym.

Where It Breathes

HANSA THAPLIYAL

Self-love is a terrace in green
And purple notes of sun after
A bath you forgot your body in
That sun in your pores begins
To make new mulch
'Lover! Lover! Lover!' fades
Outside the circle of your drying
Hair that crackles as your fingers
Slide over your warm ripe breast

A poem submitted to the Agents of Ishq annual Masturbation Shayari Contest. Hansa Thapliyal is a film-maker, teacher and animator who would like to get back to more writing.

THE ROMANCE OF FRIENDSHIP

I Have Erotic Friendships and It's Not Complicated

Was desire and sensuality only about the body?

ADITYA VIKRAM SHRIVASTAVA
9 August 2021

'Okay, but first read my letter maybe? I'm too shy to say it out loud,' Alankrita brought her hand forward, a sheet of neatly folded paper pressed between her fingers. The overcast sky roared in deep grey. Her face gave away everything that her words would proclaim later, in the sugary language of love letters. This was possibly the worst time to tell her that I was dating men, but I knew that it had now become unavoidable. So, I came out to her in haste. She snatched the paper back and tore it to pieces. I sat there, dead silent, as she recovered from her shock, until we gradually began to talk. At that time, my sexuality was a fiercely protected secret between myself and three of my very close friends. Alankrita had not been a part of that circle as I'd felt that she would break ties with me if she knew. When she finally came to know, she felt betrayed that I had deemed her unworthy of my truth; of something that I had shared with others but kept from her. It had begun to drizzle by now, and the water poured heavier as we spoke. To the passers-by, we were a boy and a girl, soggy in July rain, lodged on a green bench under a huge tree. My head was on her shoulder. For the two hours that we sat there, we received sly stares, repeated glances and a policing gaze, as any romantic couple would.

For several weeks after, Alankrita kept saying, 'I feel so foolish.' She was embarrassed because she felt she had misread the tension between us, the closeness whenever we were together. But had she been foolish? We shared the kind of trust and intimacy that she had never experienced with a straight man. We also shared a sensuousness. I liked how affectionately we touched each other. If she were a man, such physical proximity would probably have contained sexual expectations in my mind as well. Simply because we didn't enter a 'relationship' didn't mean that all that eroticism got washed away. But my coming out forced her to put our relationship in a different box—because that's how our social relationships are pre-sorted.

At the National Institute of Technology, getting 'proposed' to was a rite of passage. If a boy and a girl grew close, the slightest pull of erotic tension would be followed by the obvious next step—a proposal. Relationships were noticed and speculated about, with all kinds of gossip, because that's also how society works. Since I wasn't out as gay, it would be assumed I was straight. I soon realised that this was only a localised version of how most of the world recognised romantic coupled relationships. They were seen as the closest companionships there could be. Friendships came after that; a side dish, not the main course.

The 'friendzone' was where people imprisoned friends they did not desire, which seemed to easily mean 'undesirable'. Eroticism was not supposed to exist within a friendship. Eroticism wasn't a thing, unless it was followed by a conventional sexual act. Sex, even between conventional partners, was an obstacle course where people would cover 'bases'. Everyone swore by these rules, and tried to put things back in place when they were flouted.

With Alankrita, sensuality was now out-of-place in our relationship because I had rejected her desire to date me. To fit this new definition, our friendship shrank so much that it lost its identity, and eventually ended. But by the time Alankrita and I parted ways, my head was full of questions—when did the act of sex begin? Why was all the focus on how far we went when we were attracted to someone? What about how fully you feel? Was desire and sensuality only about the body? Was it always supposed to lead up to something carnal—a linear progression of sex—or could it exist just by itself? Why could we not imagine serious companionship with a friend? I began to think about desire itself—the emotional and physical universe within which it existed. And as I stepped further into the complex world of friendships, the way I thought about sex, desire and love changed.

After this, whenever I grew close to a girl, I would end up telling her about my sexuality. This was not only to be candid about myself and strengthen our friendship but also to pre-emptively control 'other' feelings from surfacing and floating like a sexual mist into the friendship. It was a bad attempt at trying to emulate what I imagined 'good' (read: not clouded by sexuality) friendships looked like. Then, I met Anchal.

Anchal and I met through the dramatics society, where we wrote, acted and directed together. We began to unravel ourselves freely in our daily exchanges on the way back to the hostel from rehearsal. We would go for long walks, hold hands in moments of joy, reveal secrets on tense nights, hug openly in the middle of the street, make elaborate gifts for birthdays and present each other with flirtatious compliments. I wasn't anxious when I came out to her. Like those before her, she thought that it was going to be a proposal of sorts.

But she was open in accepting what followed. 'Arey Adi, *ab saath mein ladkey taadengey!*'

The blood surged to my face when I heard her response. It felt intimate to share with her something so private, especially because we could now speak about our desires and fantasies in the company of each other. This was something I had never done with anyone earlier. I began to find more comfort in her presence because we could do all this without panicking over what our relationship was supposed to be—or not be. We were not interested in naked sex, or a sexual 'conclusion', for the lack of a better term. But the eroticism that was conceived during our moonlit walks stayed—we craved to be in physical proximity of each other, do things together, express attraction and seek each other's approval. We were often teased as a couple because that is what we were seen to be. It felt exciting to be associated with each other in that way, and we loved hearing all kinds of insinuations about us.

Anchal and I did not try to morph this into a 'sisterhood' or delete parts of our affection-attraction to fit the gay-boy-and-straight-girl friendship stereotypes. It didn't feel necessary. It didn't feel accurate. Her boyfriend would categorise us in this way. Perhaps it was denial, or perhaps it was a way to accommodate the relationship without anxiety.

It was never so with the straight men I became friends with. I had to withdraw myself from these men very soon. Even when I was simply talking to them, my brain kept playing iterations of 'mind the gap' as I spoke. It was not that mutual eroticism was missing here. I was once preparing for an improv show with a guy friend, and most scenes we played ended up becoming close encounters between us. In the course of the rehearsal, we performed a ballroom dance without knowing how it was done, breathing over each other's necks until we were almost hugging. Then we were a newly-wed couple, or a master and servant turning frisky. The practice lasted only for a few days but we continued blushing when praised by each other on social media. It felt strange that this equation stayed only as long as my sexuality was not declared. After that, the compliments stopped, and the attraction was reduced to awkward hellos in the college canteen where we couldn't entirely avoid each other. When I came out to a college junior the next year, he said, 'You're not into me, are you? I'm straight, okay?' My experience with straight men taught me that they had a lot of anxiety around handling the eroticism within a friendship. It was especially difficult when this attraction was not in tandem with the fact that they were 'straight'. They feared coming to terms with their own sexuality, which is sometimes more fluid than a sexual label can hold. It was far more ambiguous, and did not follow social rules. I did not have these conversations with them because I feared homophobia. I could get punched in the face for being 'indecent' and giving that desire a name. That being said, there were several boys in college who I became close to. Maybe they felt towards me something similar to what I felt with Anchal? But it was difficult to grapple with, since they did not have the language for it. Perhaps they did not know that eroticism could exist without sexual intercourse and could be acknowledged instead of repressed.

    My bisexual friend Suyash had had different experiences though, where eroticism made his friendship with a straight man stronger. 'I met Tanveer, and found him interesting in the beginning, but not attractive. He was also intimidating, like most cis-het men around,' Suyash told me. 'We started hanging out a lot, and then I found out that it was okay to be myself around him. That's how we got closer. Once that intimidation goes, attraction comes. Our friendship grew, in a pure-and-pious-friendship-waala way. My desire for him also grew after that. There was a situation where I had to shift residence, but I did not want to go to his flat. He eventually made me move in with him, after emotional calls and blocking all other options. 'Nahi jayega tu, aur kisi ke saath nahi jayega. Come live with me only,' he would say. I came out to him. Despite knowing that I'm attracted to him, he continued to provide comfort to me. Straight guys are generally scared away by that, but our friendship remained unchanged and full of love.'

With LGBTQ+ friends, I found it much easier to inhabit the undefined. To not name a desire or a friendship, to let them bloom together and fill the space in between. They have created a new meaning of love for me, one without inherent expectations or rules, each worthy of cherishing. I found a reflection of this in what another queer friend Raman, a law student at Gujarat National Law University, said to me about what bonds him and his female friends. 'One of my friends, she is in a different university. We are exploring. She knows I'm gay. We do every fucking thing that typical "couples" do. We are not in a relationship and she knows I'm not into girls, but she loves exploring in bed with me and I like it too. I don't know how to explain this to you, but it's a different kind of sex, not fully the physical thing. We tell each other about our hook-ups. I ask her to tell me what satisfies her, so I can make her feel good. We are very close to each other and there is no shame. Just to tell you, I'm not *itna* comfortable with guys, even though I like them sexually. But these girls are not expecting anything from me, so that makes us comfortable about our bodies. We are so open! Somewhere I feel that girls are more accepting, they are more sensitive, so even though I like guys sexually, these women are much warmer and closer to me. I don't like talking to straight guys because they always think I'm hitting on them and make fun like that. They are so fragile, so insecure about being around a gay man, because what if they like it? I have started identifying as queer now because I think my affection towards her is queer. I don't think we can set norms; that in a friendship you cannot have this or you cannot have that. It's a mutual understanding.' All friendships are different, and measuring them by the same scale doesn't help.

Anamika and Kriya, two Hijra friends from Lucknow, live that reality. '*Kabhi ye meri husband bann jati hain aur kabhi main inki husband bann jaati hu,*' remarks Kriya, wrapping their hands around Anamika's shoulders. They said that the few men who do want to have sexual relationships with them mostly want them as 'the second woman'. They are never accepted as legitimate partners, and seen as less than women because they are both from the Hijra community. There is no eroticism in their sexual relationships with men. In fact, friendship is the only relation that makes the erotic possible for them. It has not only helped them navigate the world more confidently but has also created new notions of love that are necessary for survival. How would the world, with all its regulations and norms, categorise these relationships? Are they married to each other? Or is this how friendships work? Suyash also added, 'Friendzone is such a negative term. It takes away so much from the bond I have with someone. All these terms come with their own boxes.' These boundaries give our life order, but deprive us of deeper, more complex relationships, sometimes disrespecting those bonds as less than.

I have come to understand that there are all kinds of imaginations of friendship beyond its narrow definition. Queering love means that we escape (or shun) the hierarchy of relationships and live in our own realities. Why should kissing be reserved only for romance?

What if our erotic relationships with friends are more than, or as important as sexual experiences with partners? What will it take to make space for different kinds of companionships, outside the compartments that are built for us; pleasures different from designated pleasures? What new worlds will greet us when we dare to name these 'loves'?

Aditya Vikram spends mornings writing poems in a windowless room and evenings dancing on the terrace. Most of their work revolves around the aftermath of loss, negotiations of filial love and the freedoms of queerness. They wrote this essay during an internship at Agents of Ishq.

My Mother's Lost Friendships

How can marriage and family slowly bleach friendship out of a woman's life?

RUNI

15 August 2021

I have to give the Covid-19 pandemic its due for allowing my best friend to stay in India for six months longer than anticipated. Her flight to Canada had been cancelled three times already. But the time had now come for her to leave for university in a different time zone, *saat samundar paar*. The countdown was on my Instagram stories, my calendar and in my eyes. Just say the word, and I would start bawling. My father was not home during the day, so he never witnessed these meltdowns. The night of her departure was his first sighting of my outburst. When I expected him to console me and tell me she would be back for Christmas, he just stared at me surprised, and a little disappointed. 'It's just a friend. You didn't cry this much when your brother was leaving!' I wanted to point out that my brother had only shifted to the opposite end of the same city, closer to his college. We could literally meet any time we wished to see each other—which we didn't. But I just continued to sob, too exhausted to debate. I guess I am not much of a talker in front of my father.

My best friend and I went to the same school. We knew of the other's existence as fellow batchmates for years, but didn't really interact until we applied to a summer programme together. In the process, I came across her poems and fell in love with the way she talked about the world and her space in it. It was a space I wished to occupy with her. We shared the same taste in music and films, hated our school's administration, practised our individual forms of art and rooted for each other through it all. A trip to Lodhi Garden two days after my seventeenth birthday was the first time we met outside of school, and it was the start of something new. Soon, we started to do everything together—dyed our hair, explored the majestic ruins of Delhi and mulled over our losses. What I treasured most about her was how well she understood me in times when I could not understand myself. We had major fights a couple of times a year, but always made up. Her friendship, and friendship in general for me, has been a source of unfiltered joy, sprinkled with insecurity, jealousy and friendly banter. I depend on my friends for a judgement-free corrective space. Spending time with them is not only a way for me to unwind but also to deconstruct my fixed ideas and breathe life into a side of me that often struggles to emerge.

Friendship holds different meanings for us all. I don't know where this difference stems from, but even my best friend and I do not conceive of friendship in the same way. But, despite being generations apart, my mother's interpretation of friendship and mine bear a stark resemblance.

Unlike me, my mother has three sets of friends.

First, a tight-knit group with three of her school friends. A comfort crowd, from similar social backgrounds. They meet four to five times a year and have frequent group calls where they boast about their children's achievements or bemoan their in-laws' antics.

Second, her best friend from her college days, the voice of reason to my mother's impulsive decisions. My mother, by her account, was the 'it girl' of her college days. She listened to rock music, had tonnes of junk jewellery, curly hair and the fashion sense of a designer, which she did end up becoming.

The third, her friends of convenience and circumstance. This last category includes most of the people she talks to nowadays: neighbours or mothers of my classmates. But whatever the initial intent of this friendship, the care they now have for each other is genuine. Perhaps their shared circumstances and woes help them relate to each other, and the proximity only helps.

After her marriage, my mother's first two sets of friends provided her the space to express her Punjabi self, or maybe just her essential self, away from the conservative Brahmin household she had married into. Yet, these forty-year-old women were reserved and careful with each other despite their sociable friendliness—marriage still created an undeniable gap in their relations.

Gradually, the old friendships grew cold, and new ones never had the opportunity to grow into anything more. All passion and intensity was reserved for the family. Post-marriage, my mother had been allotted one person on whom she was to depend in times of need. Extramarital emotions for friends had no space. The boxes and categories were clear and restrictive: 'You should talk to your husband about your personal problems', '*Ghar ki baat bahar mat karo*' or 'You may approach your mother but not your friends for advice on marital matters.'

Essentially, there should be no *pati, patni aur 'woh'*, even if that 'woh' is a friend. A boundary was created outside of her family unit, and friendships were supposed to be kept at a safe distance to ensure no family matters spilled over to the 'outside'. Now, she lives in a constant state of flux where one option might undermine the other. For instance, going out for lunch with friends means she can't pick my sister up from school. Living in a set-up where family takes priority over any form of social life, friendships always came second. You really can't have it all when you're a mother of three in a semi-joint conservative family.

For my father's side of the family, friendship had always been a foreign concept. And anything foreign to them meant it was unreliable. Friendships are surface-level and transactional. A dinner party for a dinner party, one formality after the other. Due to the heavy censoring imposed on them by their families, friendships never gained the same importance for them that they held for my mother and me.

Then, in 2016, my mother made a new friend, through another. Who knew forty-year-olds were capable of making best friends? Isn't friendship always associated with the young? How do you get close when you can't get reckless together? But why can't forty-year-olds be reckless, is a question I forgot to ask; the fact that my mother could be anything but my mother was unfathomable. I watched in wonder as my mother and her friend filled their days with calls of concern and laughter. They bonded over childhood experiences and trauma. She lived in the US, but my mother overcame the geographical barrier with the frequent calls and overflowing emotions. Two years into the friendship, my mother made a leap and started confiding in her about her personal life—the passing of both of my mother's parents only made their bond stronger.

But things slowly started to shift. The friend took up a risky position when she assumed the role of my mother's champion every time my parents had a clash. She became my mother's support system outside of her roles as a mother, sister, wife and daughter-in-law, and this was not well received. The point of contention now was the involvement of a stranger in our family's affairs. My mother's opinions and decisions became irrelevant, since they were all thought to be products of her friend's 'foreign' ideology. The friend became an easy scapegoat for the paternal side of the family, as all the toxicity surrounding my parents was attributed to this new stranger in my mother's life.

The question of family or friends emerged stronger than ever, and friendship was shown its place in our household, yet again. My mother is no longer in touch with that friend—an unspoken ultimatum ensured that. A relationship with a friend meant a state of domestic instability for us all. And since family, which means the family structure and not so much the people in it, must come first, the answer was obvious.

These days, Facebook posts remind her of times she can never experience again; the friendship that was strangled by the oppressive unit created by an upper-class Brahmin family's stifling norms, especially for women. I have seen my mother's highs in friendships as well as the lows for much longer than I wished for her to experience them. The loneliness is gripping, and it shows. Covid-19 only intensified this heaviness as her image was jammed into that of a *bahu*, a *biwi*, within the confines of the home. She often comes to my room, moves a few things around and sits next to me on my bed. Sometimes I respond with dry one-liners to her questions, sometimes I ask questions that she forgets to answer. There are words left unsaid, and a silence that weighs upon the both of us. I don't want to ask if she's okay. I know she is not, I just don't want to face it.

She yearns to tell me that she's lonely, scared and confused, but admitting it would make it real and complicate the relationship of parent and child. Maybe she should have listened to her wise best friend. Maybe she would have done better if she had?

I am scared for her, and for me—for the friendships that make me, me. I ache at losing that side of her; a side of airy frivolity and fun and self, that seems bleached out of the mother I now share my space with. Sometimes, I miss her. Other times, I try to make her forget.

Runi is an artist and pianist from New Delhi who hopes to occupy a tiny space at the intersection of behavioural economics and art. When not watching mukbangs online, she can be found curating a list of the best tiramisu places in town. She wrote this essay during an internship with Agents of Ishq.

You Are My Di!

What keeps an intense friendship alive in a world that defines love and friendship separately?

PRAVEENA SHIVRAM
4 August 2021

At a friend's place, two gin and tonics down, senses lulled enough to float through the space of the unsaid, the unbidden, legs stretched out on the blue couch, faintly dusted with dog and cat hair, feet being massaged by another friend as she scolds me for how tight they are. In that space, that oasis of silence, she asks me, 'Do you think in an alternate universe, Neha and you might have been lovers?'

It comes like a comet streaking across the sky, the tail bright and beautiful. Not the thought, no—I have heard this line so many times in the twenty-one years of knowing and loving Neha—rather, the idea, momentarily slicing through my sky … the idea of an alternate universe where perhaps love could be defined in another way. That idea was electrifying.

☙

I have always wondered, what does it mean to be in love? What separates the idea of love from friendship? Does it always have to be reduced to a potent concentrate of physicality and sexuality that can then, over time, be diluted? We are a country where it isn't uncommon to see friends of the same sex holding hands and walking down the road, their bodies plastered to each other as they go zipping down the roads in their two-wheelers—even as gay rights and acceptance continue to inhabit an uneasy space.

I grew up like most people with the binaries of gender and identity, where discovering who you were was intrinsically tied to how and who we love. Anything that fell between that inchoate space of friendship and love was to be quickly categorised or swiftly denied. It is the binaries that exist in hushed whispers, as if uttering them somehow wakes up the slumbering air of gossip—*You're acting like you are obsessed. You need to stop talking to her for a week; do it like a test, to see if you can.*' 'Who do you love more? Me or Neha? This is not feeling like a normal friendship to me.' 'Look at them, they're like girlfriend and boyfriend. It's gross.'

———

I met her in college. She was one year my junior, and we were both pursuing a degree in English literature. The all-women college I was a part of, after twelve years of co-ed schooling, felt oddly refreshing, liberating even, because of the complete absence of male attention. We had a newly-introduced credit system, the choice of electives to both first- and second-year students. I was stuck with biology. Ten minutes after class began and we had all settled in, Neha walked in: short hair, round glasses, a mole on her face. She was wearing black jeans and an oversized check shirt (making her look shorter and rounder than she was) and had a tall guitar case slung across her shoulder. She almost looked like a boy. She sat right in the front.

That same afternoon, I saw her at the auditions for the Western Music Club. I was already part of the Light Music

Club. In Madras, the term 'light music' is used to define the music from our movies. To denote that which is obviously different from the heavier classical repertoire of Carnatic/Hindustani music, the notes settling around your feet like cement, demanding your full and complete attention. Light music, on the other hand, was a lot more generous, a lot more lenient. You could commit the sacrilege of walking away halfway.

I auditioned with Celine Dion's 'My Heart Will Go On', a song already scratchy from the number of times I had listened to it on my Walkman. I was not selected. Neha, though, was.

Somewhere between my second year and her first year, we met. Properly. *'Have you heard Neha play the guitar and sing? Oh you must!'* And so, led by other friends, I made my way to her at break time, outside the canteen under the big banyan tree, that she would later teach me to climb, holding my hand, guiding my steps. I discovered the warmth of her hands. I also discovered Simon and Garfunkel, CSNY, Cat Stevens, Bread and so many others through her.

Somewhere between my third year and her second year, when she became the president of the Western Music Club and I was finally selected (ha!), we spent countless hours of rehearsals in her house, as a group and alone, when I learnt to play the guitar—she the tutor, me the student. I spent nights in her house—the two of us sharing a blanket, looking at the glow worms and the stars and the moon stuck on her ceiling, sharing stories of family, of history, of grief, of pain and love. I melded into the rhythm of her life, her home, her family— we could no longer separate time spent together and time spent apart. Somewhere between these moments, I became her music and she mine.

I rediscovered the art of letter-writing with Neha. We would write to each other constantly. Long letters. She still holds the record—fifty-two pages, front and back. I was swept into this world of antiquity and charm, of magic and make-believe, of finding letters snuck into post boxes or slipped under the door. When I left for Bombay, for my post-graduate diploma, the letters I received almost every week became my anchor against Bombay's unforgiving harshness and the terrifying need to grow up. Amidst the thousands rushing to catch the train, I was just one more, being shoved and nudged, and shoving and nudging in turn, and yet, I was different. I had Neha's letters. In one, she said, 'I am sending you a musc grave.' When the next letter arrived, it had five dead mosquitoes stuck under transparent cello tape. It was amusing then—we battle mosquitoes in Madras every monsoon, countless killed without second thought—but in retrospect, it was an offering, a sacrifice of blood, seeping through the layers of devotion, of a friendship entering the nebulous space of love undefined. And so viscerally different from the other friendships in my life that, however close, never demanded so much of me.

A year later, I would violently shun this as another intense relationship would take hold of my life—the clearly defined 'lover' relationship—and I would let Neha go. Not gracefully, of course not. But with the anger of an avenging tribal chief—my swords were out, my armour in place, my eyes blazing, my words a rain of pins. The onslaught was brutal, I couldn't control it. Stormy phone conversations; loud bangs of the landline phone; directed, deliberate and furious silences when in a group gathering, making everyone uncomfortable; a constant need to attack. It was confusing, especially because I never knew what I was fighting—my own incapability of rising beyond definitions (who is Neha, now that I have a boyfriend?), or my inability to fully succumb to them?

It felt like ancient anger, the other side of unconditional love, the depths of an almost satanic urge to see how far she would go in her love, how far I would go in my anger and if we would come out the other side. Friendship often accords that exit card; the stakes are never high enough and the platitudes many—*things change; it is natural to drift apart when life takes over; it's hard to maintain close friendships; we picked up exactly where we left off*—unlike a lover who would demand redemption—*if you love me, you will forgive me.*

It was like I was standing on a faraway mountain watching Neha try and build a bridge from the opposite end, deeply relieved that she was willing to cross the rapidly growing chasm but also unable to stop myself from burning it down each time.

Years later, between her marriage and my divorce, we would talk about this several times over. When I would ask her what made her stay, she would simply say, 'Because I love you.' In her forgiveness I would find myself again.

※

Soon after we met in college, we went on our first turtle walk along the Besant Nagar beach, where turtle conservationists take a small group of people for a walk under the moonlight to save nests from poachers. Neha had brought her guitar along. On one of the rest stops along the way, she played her music. Once we reached the hatchery, a good four hours later, we all spread our sheets on the sand and fell asleep, waking up to a stunning sunrise marred by some bums along the shore taking a shit.

That morning, still heady from the salt and sand in our souls, we decided to walk back home, about six kilometres. At 6.30 a.m., after a quick cup of tea from a roadside stall, we began heading home, the roads relatively empty. Half an hour later, still nowhere close to home, the traffic now surging past us, I can't remember what it is we talked about, or even the exhaustion of the walk under Madras' relentless sun, both of us taking turns to carry the guitar, but I remember as we neared my house, we found a tree. The trunk of this tree was almost touching the ground before the branches lifted it up to meet the sky. We named this tree Lyd and it became, in many ways, the symbol of our friendship—we would return to it when we fought, or when we wanted to meet in between errands. But that first time, as we sat in a flushed silence, we felt that tingle of acceptance surge upward from the base of our spines, that blot of recognition spreading into an unrecognisable shape in our hearts—I see you and you see me, though we are not lovers. We did not inscribe our initials on that trunk. We did not need to.

During the Year of the Big Separation, when I went to Bombay, Neha would surprise me with a five-day visit. She would sit in the playground on campus as I finished my classes and then we would take the bus or the train together to see not the sights that Bombay had to offer but the paths I walked every day. When Neha left, I accompanied her to the station. We hugged outside, lingering just a bit longer, and the auto drivers around us hooted. Maybe what they saw was the physical hug, but what we felt was the comfort of all of our silences that had and would punctuate our conversations, held together by two bodies.

On one of the many afternoons I spent at Neha's after college, we came up with a secret world—Bob, we called it—so we could escape into it whenever we wanted to. We never gave it a definitive form then (we drew it like an amoeba) but twenty-one years later, I think that amoeba-shaped world managed to fit into this one, precisely because it had the ability to keep changing and growing.

'Are you my sister, or my friend, or are you my "di"?' Neha's daughter asks mine, in between a game they are playing. They are the same age, my daughter younger than Neha's by two-and-a-half months. In Tamil, 'di' (pronounced 'dee') is a colloquial suffix added to the ends of sentences between female friends, and yet, like the language itself, it carries a complexity; this word between the Hindi *dosti* and *yaari*, between the sky that can contain the nuance of every word uttered and the sky that can be relentless in its chaos of understanding. My daughter replies with a laugh, 'I am your di,' and it strikes me that perhaps that is what Neha is to me as well. My di. Two letters that straddle the sides of friendship and love, like a fearless warrior, hands on her hips, legs splayed, unwavering eyes meeting the world and absolving it of its own disdain. Two letters that become the womb of nebulous meaning, shielding us from the stubborn import of definitions. Two letters that did not need an alternate universe to survive in. After all, it could in fact birth new ones.

Praveena Shivram is an independent writer based in Madras. You can read her work here: www.praveenashivram.com.

Love was a Stereotype. Friendship was Radical. And Then, I Met Her

If witnessing a relationship slowly die out like a star collapsing into itself were a colour, it would be tangerine

NAMRATA MUKHERJEE

5 August 2023

Last Christmas, we met for the first time after speaking over text for over six months. She came to visit me. We walked around, sat on swings in a park and spoke in measured tones, the awkwardness of our first meeting melting away like the remaining specks of sunshine on a December evening. As she was leaving, and I followed her down the stairs, she turned and tried to kiss me on the cheek. Shocked, I lost my balance and tumbled down the stairs. As she apologised, helping me to my feet, my spiralling anxiety about a potential Covid-19 infection was suspended. In a split second my mask was off, and I exclaimed impatiently, 'Fuck it, kiss me!' Six months of pent-up desire culminated in us kissing on a precarious staircase and awkwardly groping each other as we tried to make the best of those thirty seconds.

It's been a year, it's Christmas again—and we don't talk anymore. Two days ago, I sent her a text, ending things. The sky was tangerine. The sun sank into the pits of despair as a cold winter evening descended on me.

With the Fags, It Always Starts with Instagram

I'd returned home from New York at the beginning of the pandemic. Little did I know that the year and a half I would be at home would end up being one of the most hellish periods of my life. People I loved died. People I loved shrank. And my girlfriend of four years and I decided to finally call it quits. Amidst the grief, I lost myself and spent hours on the Internet. I also joined a queer writing group—the one thing that saved me from myself.

I first came across her on a queer Instagram page where she had written about her identity. From there, I followed her on her personal page. And then began what would be, for the longest time, a one-sided longing—thirsty, filthy, escapist. I was shockingly horny and throbbing for her. Breathing in and out during yoga classes, I imagined her eating me out on my mat. One desperate day, I crawled into her DMs, responding to her tirade about bottoms. 'Power bottom here,' I texted, in a moment of rare courage, and she responded. After that, I kept making pathetic attempts to catch her attention, but she didn't particularly reciprocate. And that was the reason for our first, albeit one-sided, fight.

I resented her for the lack of attention. At the same time, I memorised her Instagram posts. 'All desire is heterosexual,' she stated in one. 'Punish me like a straight girl,' I pined. Soon enough, I found myself talking about her during the weekly writing group meetings. After all, us city queers are defined by six degrees of separation. And in a moment of euphoria, Z, a friend from my writing group, told me that the girl had recently broken up with her partner and was probably single. Fuck yeah!

With Fags, Hinge is the Lord and Saviour

Sitting in my room, in a city far from hers, I hedged my bets. She was recently single. Single people go on dating apps, right? So, I changed my location to where she was—a city I would not step foot in for several months.

She showed up almost immediately. I stayed glued to her profile, refusing to budge but also refusing to initiate. 'Oh hello, look who's here,' came her message. And over the next several days we exchanged streams of texts.

Her: You're the most interesting person I have met here in a while.
Me: I won't be in [your city] for another few months.
Her: It's okay.
Me: I don't date.
Her: I'm good with that; I am not looking to date either.

Our texts continued for around five months. One day she slipped in a sext.

I resisted, given the virginal sexter I was, but finally gave in and sent her a picture of me shirtless, my dark hair cascading down my shoulders. Desire is a relentless thirst. Over the next few months, we spoke every day. From aggressive sexting we moved to tender check-ins, narratives about our histories and anecdotes about our lives. I told her I was polyamorous, and my idea of intimacy involved not distinguishing between romantic and non-romantic relationships. She said that this idea was new to her. Monogamy was all that she had known, and she drew a clear distinction between partners and friends. But then neither of us were out to date, right? So, our ideological mismatches would not matter, right? As the days passed, we became a daily presence in each other's lives.

We would occasionally chat about our pandemic days, but mostly we would work together in silence over video calls. Slipping glances and smiling at each other across 1,500 kilometres. Only blue skies, no tangerine.

Fags Are Doomed to Be Lonely

I was moving to the middle of nowhere for a new job, and she was moving too. It was meant to be. And so, I arrived in her city, excited about my newfound freedom. We spent a night at an Airbnb on our first 'date'. She gave me a book by Akwaeke Emezi. I was the favourite thing to happen to her in 2021, her note said. As she stood semi-naked freezing after her bath, I wrapped her with a towel and held her till she stopped shivering. She finally felt happy, she said.

Same, man, same. On our first day at my new place in the middle of nowhere, we cleaned the house and fucked the night away. We got defrauded of a shitload of money on our second. Spent our third at the police station lodging a useless criminal complaint. And when she left, I awaited her return. Longing is an instrument played till your fingers bleed. Soon, she moved to the middle of nowhere. She would come over, and we would speak about gender, our exes, our work, our friends, things that broke us and made us. We spoke a lot about our conflicting ideas of intimacy. She identified as a hopeless romantic. I, as an eye-rolling cynic.

She used the word 'love' even before we had met. For me, the word carried weight. It meant commitment, work, a learning curve. I used the word too, though much later. We talked about bodies, her transness and my newfound transness. And we kissed and fucked a lot. We also told each other we loved each other, a lot, a lot. But as time passed, and work overtook our lives, we texted less and her visits became sporadic. No one was to blame, but it didn't matter. It bothered me. I texted her often. When she found the time, she would respond.

Me: Hey, can you come over this Thursday evening?
Her: Hey, no, I'm stretched really thin and have a lot of work.
Me: Okay.

Okay? This was not a part of the plan—my new life was supposed to mirror perfection. And as I sat alone in my balcony overlooking naked fields, the sky was tangerine. By the end of the first month, I started growing disillusioned with my job, the middle of nowhere and the slow metamorphosis of our relationship. I missed my friends and everything the big city offered.

My days consisted of working alone in a dilapidated apartment that overlooked endless dark fields, catching a sad bus to my workplace and returning home to sit on my pot and smoke a cigarette. One cigarette turned into two. Two into three. Three into as many as I needed to fill the empty pockets of my life. In *Lonely City*, Olivia Lang writes that loneliness feels like being hungry, when everyone around you is readying for a feast. I was starving. And as much as I tried exorcising the ghost of loneliness, I found myself mutating into an unrecognisable person. And so, I turned to her for solace. Insisting she come meet me more often. She did her best. But something had changed. She'd come, we'd hang out and fuck, and then she would fall off the face of the Earth. I would text her every day, only to be met with delayed sporadic responses.

It was only when we sexted that her responses flooded my phone. Suddenly, our relationship felt like a transaction that would repeat itself with her arrival and departure. I realised I was trying to flee my loneliness, and that she was my destination. I wrote her a measured email. 'I love our time together,' it said. 'But I also feel like once you leave, you leave.' And so, I asked her for space, such that I could work myself out of the habit of an oppressive dependence on her. 'I also think perhaps we should stop sleeping with each other. Because honestly, it makes me feel a little used at times,' I added. She wrote back the same night, apologising and acknowledging her shortcomings. She was stretched thin and had a lot going on, she wrote. Her email was kind, an honest acknowledgement of what she could and couldn't offer. 'I'm also sorry that the sex made you feel used. It was out of sheer love and desire,' she added. We decided to not text for the next few months so I could unlearn my unhealthy dependence on her. Everything I despised about romantic love and mandatory monogamy, I now imbibed.

My politics on intimacy dripped away like a leaking faucet. But after a day of silence came her text. She had spent the day trying her best to distract herself but soon she found herself returning to me. And in that moment, my fragile will was broken. 'I love you.' 'I love you too.'

Where Are All My Lesbians?

In *Thirteen Ways to Love*, there is a story titled 'Where Are All My Lesbians?' The author writes about her break-up and uses the phrase 'queer fragility' to describe the precarity of lesbian relationships. The first time I read it, I despised it. The second time, I was lonely in the middle of a brutal New York winter, and my trysts with queer dating hadn't really led anywhere. I still found her pining annoying, but I was more empathetic. Today, I am terrified of reading it.

Fucking queer fragility. And what kind of lesbian was I anyway? Being lesbian is a political identity, as poet and essayist Adrienne Rich argued in *Compulsory Heterosexuality and Lesbian Existence*. In pop culture, lesbians are unhinged, co-dependent, hopeless romantics and, honestly, sort of pathetic. Anyway, I was sort of an Adrienne Rich lesbian, or so I believed.

'Not all feelings are valid,' I would exclaim to her. 'I don't get this lesbian obsession with coupling up in the bat of an eyelid. Why are we such stereotypes?'

'Friendships are radical, I don't do well with hierarchising intimacies. I despise romantic love—it is so shallow and vacuous. I intellectually disagree with it,' I would tell her animatedly.

How the tables turn—I'm a pop culture lesbian now.

On the Right to Rage

On the right to rage, I am a lawyer by training and so are most of my friends. We read and discuss critical legal theory which rightfully calls out the law for all its pitfalls. The most popular discourse is a critique of rights. 'Is there a right to sex?' ponders philosopher Amia Srinivasan in a famous essay. In *Gender, Alterity and Human Rights*, Ratna Kapur argues, 'On some level, our rights-related liberal projects are on life support and further palliation is pointless.' Denying a right to marriage to the queers (largely cis-gay savarnas) violates the equality code, argue petitioners in our courts. But fuck all that! Is there a right to rage? I mean, of course there is—rage is political and powerful and can overthrow oppressive empires. But I wonder whether we have a right to rage against lovers. Rage that seeks to shock the lover's system into acknowledging (and meeting) one's needs as opposed to measured conversations and therapy speak. Is that right to rage (vis-à-vis our lovers) accompanied by the right to be verbally cruel? Most crucially, is that right accompanied by a guarantee to be forgiven by the lover once the storm calms? One baffling night, in the pits of despair, I exercised my assumed right to rage.

I never addressed the principal question: Was she my lover? Was I hers? After all, we weren't dating. Didn't matter.

I gave into my base impulse, and without warning, sent her paragraph after paragraph of accusatory angry texts. Everything is on your terms. Everything. When we talk, how we talk, how often we talk, when I can see you, when we fuck. You only respond consistently when we sext. My needs and expectations never matter. You disappear on me all the time. Weapons drawn, I ambushed her and accused her of breaking my heart.

A friend read my texts and responded with a measured, 'Hmm. So, what do you think you will get out of this?' She added, 'She is immediately going to go into defensive mode. Did you really achieve anything?' Another friend firmly believed that there is a right to rage at the lover. 'Of course!' she exclaimed. 'Get mad, be cruel, be angry, say those nasty words out loud.' After all, what is a lover but a receptacle for our grief? And so, I exercised my right to rage, and she exercised her right to retreat. She shut down. Shut me out. And the brutal silence hung between us like a thick fog. Tangerine.

The Vanishing Self

After weeks of silence, as the anger settled and desperation crept in, I wrote to her. I apologised profusely and begged for another chance. 'Intimacy is the only thing I value,' I said. 'And it's the only thing I am willing to fight for.' She took her time, but eventually we started speaking. In a week, I was headed back to my hometown for over a month, and so we agreed to meet. We met in a restaurant designed for heady first dates, rather than difficult fall-out conversations. I apologised and promised to do better. After our meal, I went home with her, and we fucked all night long. As she lay on top of me, she paused, looked bewildered and said, 'Fuck, I'm in love with you.'

'I'm in love with you too,' I responded. 'But I am also often in love with my friends,' I added. And she sat silently with that, before she ate me out.

All desire is political, but sometimes, when people tell you that they are in love with you, one must resist the urge to reduce that moment to a political project. 'I am in love with you too,' is all that was necessary. And in a few days, I flew away, 1,500 kilometres separating us once again, her teeth marks all over my collarbones, memories that I desperately clung onto as they slowly faded away.

Does the Label Make It Taste Better?

Still with me? Well then, let's skip the mundane details of a month-and-a-half of distance. Suffice to say, we broke each other, in ways I could not fathom possible.

We argued and hurt and misunderstood—an endless cycle of disappointment, anger and exhaustion repeating itself. One day, after a charged exchange, I blocked her on Instagram. At this point, I unabashedly acknowledge my role in sabotaging the relationship. I didn't want to date her as an antidote for my loneliness. But then why do people date, if not to avoid being alone in this world meant for two? She wanted to speak in person about what had ensued. When I returned, she wasn't ready. And so, I drove to the middle of nowhere, and for over a month, there was complete silence from her end. Every day I shrank a little more, consumed by her loss. By now, there was very little keeping me motivated at work. I hated the middle of nowhere and my health gave way.

My depression and anxiety had returned with a vengeance. I once rejoiced in my singlehood, but now I longed, hesitantly though, for the comfort of coupledom. 'I am in love with you, and I am ready to do the work of repair,' is what I longed to say to her. I woke up every morning and vomited into my toilet before catching my sad yellow bus to work. And I came home, smoked and repeatedly checked our WhatsApp chat. Online. Offline. Online. Offline. Silence.

One day, I erased all our WhatsApp messages from my phone. But I emailed myself a copy. Thus, in my email somewhere lies an archive—over 100 pages of texts between two fags exchanged over a period of a year or so—of falling and failing. And then, one day she broke her silence—with the terms of a relationship that could be possible between us. A checklist of things she could offer and could not. An essay about all the ways I'd hurt her. I apologised and agreed to her checklist, without caveat. I wanted her back, and I acknowledged my faults, but in this process, I disappeared— my hurt no longer mattered. My grievances, locked away, gathering dust. Finally, she came to see me and spent the night at my place. She behaved as if nothing had happened between us. I resisted the engraved instinct to kiss her. She kept hugging me, kissing my hand, touching me all over. And I gave in. And old patterns repeated themselves.

Except something was different. It was like a part of her had checked out. But I, who had no right to rage any longer and had made the mistake of saying out loud 'but sometimes I am also in love with my friends,' must make amends. So, I walked on eggshells around her, agreeing to all her terms, caveating every text I sent to her with 'you don't have to respond'/'only if you have bandwidth and want to'/'prioritise yourself'. The desire was gone. The hunger, gone. The intimacy, gone. The effort, unrequited. The nudes, given polite responses. Blocks of text from my end, met with a line or two. The sex followed, once again, by a disappearing act. In 'We Ain't Together', King Princess sings, 'We say, "I love you," but we ain't together/Do you think labels make it taste much better?'

She tells me she wished I hadn't followed my confession of being in love with her with the addendum that I am also in love with my friends.

'It's not the same for me,' she said. 'I love my friends but it's not the same as being in love.' 'But why does it matter that sometimes I am in love with my friends?' I ask her. 'If I give you everything you need from a partnership, should that fact matter?' 'Yes,' she says. 'It does.' But then what's the point of being queer, I wondered. Aren't we supposed to do better than the straights? Isn't queerness more about how we arrange our intimacies? 'Gender is not a binary,' the queers scream, but love is? 'I don't think we'd be good if we dated.'

'I feel like you don't see me,' she said in response to one of my texts about us exploring dating. Over another conversation, she claimed, 'I don't think I can meet your needs.' Another night: 'I think you see me better than you did before.' Of course I did. Because for three months, it was all I worked towards. Loving her in ways she wanted to be loved. Texting her, on her terms. Meeting her, on her terms. I did everything possible to 'see' her—till I vanished. 'I am so confused, you're so contradictory,' I told her one day. 'I am not saying we should date, but I am not sure what the reason is.'

'Is it that I don't "see" you? Is it because I am sometimes in love with my friends? Is it because you think you can't meet my needs?' I reply. Internally, I scream. *WHAT THE FUCK IS IT?*

'All these things can be true at the same time,' she says. One night, the last time we met each other, she came over and told me about how she and a gorgeous queer ('T') have developed romantic feelings for each other. They discussed it, she says, but decided not to date because they didn't want to risk the friendship and were not mentally ready to be romantically entangled. A part of me died. *Pick me, choose me,*

I wanted to beg, but I only listened as she pottered around the kitchen talking about T. 'I feel threatened,' I told her. But I stopped there. And as we lay next to each other, I said, 'I need to let you go, but before that I need to know that you're no longer in love with me—are you?'

She was thoughtful. 'I fell in love with you, but not in that way. I always held back because you were so clear about not wanting to date.'

'Okay, so just to make this clear, you are no longer in love with me, right?'

'I love you, but I am not in love with you.'

We fell silent. 'I guess I am still grieving you, you know,' she says. I have no fucking idea what that means so I press her a bit more. She gives me vague responses, punctured by even more vague silences. And so, I give myself permission to cry in front of her. 'Why are you still sleeping with me?' I ask her.

'Because I like you, and I am attracted to you.'

These words would come back to shatter me, irreparably. They made me feel disposable, replaceable, forgettable. Despite this, I rode her hard that night. She never really let me top, and despite me being a vers, we always had sex with her exclusively topping. But I didn't give a fuck that night, and so I instructed her to sit up, topped her and rode her till she gasped, breathless. She left and then her Instagram was flooded with posts about T. I followed them both. And boy, were they at it—public declarations of love and admiration. 'This is my favourite picture,' T commented on one of her posts about them. 'Arrey, you are my fav!' she replied.

It's no longer 2021, and she never promised I'd still be her favourite in 2022. One aching night, she posted a picture of T sitting on her desk at 1 a.m. I had a meltdown, called my ex-girlfriend and sobbed. 'How did she move on so fast?' I wept. 'Am I that forgettable, that difficult?' Is this our legacy—a war-torn landscape of haggard emotions?

Endnotes
Oh, by the way, I quit my job and decided to move back home.
12 December 2022

Me: Give me a yes or no answer, okay. When I come back to the city, is there any chance for us to give us a shot?

Her: … I really don't know, and I think I really don't want to be romantically entangled for a significant while and recuperate. That's the honest answer.

Tangerine.
14 December 2022

Me: At the cost of sounding annoying, if you and T are heading somewhere, do let me know … very hard for me to witness you moving on … given I am still grieving you.

Her: As far as T is concerned, she is a dear friend more than anything.

More than anything.

Tangerine.
23 December 2022; 12.09 p.m.

Her (responding to a text about meeting before I leave): I can't do earlier to be entirely honest. I still have [work] to finish and I'm coming down with a fever from exhaustion.

Me: Do you wanna take a rain check?

Tangerine.
23 December 2022; 1.51 p.m.

Me: I am calling … quits. Having reflected on the past year, I don't think there is any future for us, even in the realm of friendship. So, I am out.

Her: Alright. I'm not going to argue with that.

Tangerine.
23 December 2022 onwards

Me:
Her:

Tangerine.
This is my story. It is not our story. Neither is it hers.

Namrata is a queer lawyer who lives and works in Delhi and Kolkata.

Body and Other Requirements for Sex

ADITI GHATOLE

Vaginas are beautiful
So are dicks
Full asses and slender bums
Take your pick.
Pot bellies are sensual
Flat tummies are 'in'
Belly rolls are welcome here
Having a body ain't a sin.
Penises long or slender
Breasts soft and tender
For some chemistry, we vouch!
In the bedroom or the couch!
Regardless of what you say
The clitoris is the best
On lonesome nights, on shitty days
It's a worthy little quest.
With him or her
Gendered or queer
A marriage or a date
Experience only makes it better, mate!
We love the grabbing and
The handful of squeezing. But ...
We know. Making love
Ain't always easy!
So, we help each other quench the thirst,

With bodies ... spread apart
And we learn to love ourselves first!
Each piece, each broken part.

Aditi Ghatole is a wannabe BomBae from Nagpur. An असभ्य औरत *also know as the hysterical woman.*

UNDOING THE WORLD

Diary of An Indian Sex Educator

It was a co-ed school. But the boys were not going to learn about the body

SRINIDHI RAGHAVAN

31 July 2017

Her: Is it possible for you to talk on menstruation and child sexual abuse to young kids?
Me: Sure! How old are they?
Her: Studying in class five and six.
Me: Great! That shouldn't be a problem.
Her: There is one thing though—you can't talk about sex.

An awkward silence followed. I had no choice but to agree.
 This was my first encounter with sex-ed.
 I had been working with a feminist organisation in Hyderabad for a year then. I was twenty-four years old, trained in legal rights, human rights and legislations, but had not started training in sex, sexuality or reproductive health. Those were reserved for experienced trainers. The conversation mentioned above was merely an introduction to the long list of conditions sex educators must work with.
 To prepare for this class, in a private school in a posh part of the city, I spent two weeks reading. I read about the

human body. I studied how the parts looked. I read books for kids, for adults, for trainers, for teachers all in the hope that I would find the language to talk about sex without talking about sex. I worried about the language I could use. I worried about the details I could go into. I worried about the questions the girls would raise. A colleague advised me to stop fretting so much and just be honest and tell them everything I knew.

I walked into a classroom full of excited ten- to twelve-year-old girls armed with illustrations, stories and honesty.

Yes, only girls.

It was a co-ed school. But the boys were not going to learn about the body.

An illustrated and simple path was used to explain the body to them. We had two hours to ourselves. They asked questions about bodily changes. I responded to them as simply as I could, trying to conceal my uncertainty. To add to my unease, female teachers sat around the classroom like the word police to monitor every word I used.

But I'd survived my first session.

After that first experience, I got more relaxed at doing sex-ed classes. I realised how relevant it was for girls (and boys!). I struggled trying to explain sex without saying sex. But in order to conduct this session, we negotiated to do a free one on gender, with both boys and girls from an older age group. The hope was that we would be able to touch some more complex issues as well, while staying away from the word 'sex'.

One day a young girl from the same school came up to me after class. 'Ma'am, there is a girl in my class who's had …' Her voice drifted off. She obviously had been warned to not say the word. I was terrified. How will I respond to her without using the forbidden word? What was I supposed to ask her now? Where were these kids having sex without any adult catching them?

I found the words to ask her how she knew. She said she had seen them. The imagery that flooded my brain in those moments is hard to pen down. To be honest, I was shocked and worried for her and for the children she had seen engaging in the act. These kids were, after all, just ten. Seeing two people have sex must have raised all kinds of questions! But how could I even ask further?

After a few moments of silence, I summoned the courage to ask her to describe what she saw. When she explained, I realised she hadn't seen them have sex but kiss. I was relieved. But kissing was also a taboo subject I was not allowed to address. I struggled to find words to help ease her worries and reassure her that they weren't actually having sex.

To explain menstruation or puberty, and not how sex or reproduction works means that young girls and boys often have no idea HOW the sperm enters the female body. In their minds, it could have travelled through the mouth!

Till, of course, they discover the Internet or maybe porn.

As I continued on the path of sex education, it only got more complicated. This wasn't an isolated experience where sex educators are encouraged to talk about menstruation, health, child sexual abuse and even violence without bringing up sex. We can explain the process of menstruation without talking about the male parts or male functions. But every time I left it at, 'When the sperm fertilises the egg,' a hand would go up in class. 'But how?'

I learnt that their curiosity and questions were not the only things I would have to tackle. We used illustrations while talking about the body, sex and sexuality because we felt it would be easier to digest these concepts this way.

Once my colleague and I were training a group of eighty women on sexual and reproductive rights in Hyderabad. There were women of all age groups, married, unmarried, young, sexually active, not active yet, the whole spectrum. We began with a few exercises through mapping the sexual and reproductive parts of the human body.

It took us more than an hour just to get the parts of the body down on the chart paper. Many of them were not named and the shapes were unknown. Most of the women and girls didn't know about the several orifices in the female body. Ovaries were the easiest to name. Fallopian tubes existed somewhere in that area. The vagina and uterus were hard to differentiate. They beat around the bush when asked about female pleasure. Anger, hate and pain were easier to pinpoint on the body. Pleasure and joy were more difficult. Giggles were the most common response to any question.

They had trouble using the word 'penis', forget drawing it. We moved on by showing illustrations with close-ups of the body parts, particularly sexual body parts. We also circulated a labelled drawing of the female sexual parts to show the many different parts of the body. To our surprise, one of the girls in the front row began to weep. I nudged my colleague who continued the class as I led the girl outside the classroom.

Talking about the body, I have learnt, can lead to varied experiences. The young girl confessed that she had never seen a picture of a penis before. It was overwhelming for her. She told us that it was not like what she imagined or knew, and was shaken by the open conversation we were attempting.

⸎

I was unnaturally nervous when I had to address my first mixed gender group. I had fallen deep into a comfort zone of only addressing same-sex groups. I was reminded of my own biology class on reproduction. My teacher made little or no eye contact with us. We all giggled.

Not making eye contact was just like talking about menstruation but not sex.

But I had learnt that eye contact helped. And one could talk about sex while having to talk about something else.

It was a week-long course at a college. HIV/AIDS was the chosen topic. We had to talk about it (without talking about sex, remember!). The only relief was there weren't any teachers in the room. After breaking up the class into small groups, we handed out sheets of paper on HIV/AIDS and sneakily added in questions on sex, sexuality and masturbation. The questions were provocative, attempting to break myths about masturbation as well as sexual pleasures. The effect was beautiful. The class was initially shy, but as they realised this was a non-judgmental space, they began to discuss how no one had ever talked about masturbation above a whisper. After their group work, we addressed the questions together. Some of them more vocal than the others, but questions were answered in loud cheers of yes and no!

'Is masturbation dirty?'

'No.'

'Can we have sex during the menstrual cycle?'

'Yes.'

'Condoms are a hundred per cent effective.'

'No.'

It was one of my most open and honest experiences during sex-ed. Students expressed how no one had ever spoken to them openly about sex, which had led to several misconceptions, especially around the female body and pleasure. The sessions helped me see that it is never too late for a proper sex-ed class—as long as the space is open for safe, explorative and constructive discussion, all words can be used. Unfortunately, the next day, when they discussed the class with their political sciences teacher, I received a look of disapproval from her.

But I did not make eye contact. I just smiled to myself.

Srinidhi is a disabled feminist, writer, researcher and educator. She works at the intersections of sexuality, gender, disability and technology. She has worked with young persons, parents, caregivers, women across ages, educators, women's rights, feminist and disability rights organisations for over a decade.

Unfuckable Me

'You're not like other girls.'

ALIZA KHAN

13 February 2017

A self-styled Adonis recently told me that he has never really been attracted to Indian women or short girls, but that I'm just so beautiful, he feels especially drawn to me. That, as a short Indian girl, I was somehow different from other short Indian girls was an arbitration he felt perfectly comfortable vocalising as he was thinking through it—an articulation imbued with the expectation that when a rich, handsome boy tells a girl she's pretty, she is going to listen.

I laughed at that comment for hours. To what should I compare this? Probably to the moment when a twenty-one-year-old girl with a Twitter account dedicated to the Indian Minister of Road Transport and Highways woke up to a tweet from him announcing that he was going to inaugurate a toll booth in Ghaziabad in her honour. When you are confronted with something this ridiculous, you begin to recognise the social forces and emotional anchors that undergird such interactions. You sometimes need things to get really weird before you can notice them. Flirting is about flair, about expression, but pay attention to most of the flirting you're at the receiving end of and you can see what's actually going on: exceptionalisation.

Are you even desirable as a heterosexual woman if men can't describe you as an exception?

When I was sixteen, a guy seven years older than me told me he liked me because I was smarter and more mature than women his age.

My high school boyfriend told me that he liked me not only because I was 'pretty, smart and funny' (teenage male thinking is remarkably complex) but also because I was the ONLY girl he knew who was all three of those things. He was a top athlete in school, so you know, only such an exceptional girl was worthy of the boy.

One of the more boring qualities of girlhood is that the desire you experience is predicated on the desire you produce. It was as if this male X-ray romantic vision was what discovered me, like the diamond in the rough that I was. Being the object of male desire became a way for me to understand my own brilliance because male biases are thought of as unassailable facts.

This feeling of desirability was mapped onto the otherwise competitive, jaggedly antagonistic dynamics with the boys I went to school with. In class nine, I complained to my school counsellor that a boy in my class threw a razor blade at me, and she said, 'He comes from a conservative Brahmin family and isn't used to a Muslim girl getting more marks than him—also, he probably thinks you're pretty.'

As I grew older, I figured out that I couldn't make the jokes about my body hair or my father being a member of the Taliban (*just kidding, yaar*) go away, so I decided to be the best in whatever I could be the best in, which was many things. Boys considering me pretty felt like another victory, like I was queen bee of the wolfpack or something similarly muddled.

This projected self-image operated through a fragile sense of my own girlhood. I believed that I had transcended the *funda* of being a girl—because apparently something about me was too scary, too strange. I've always struggled with the idea that I was meant to be a girl or that I am too much of a girl in the first place. I am an unremarkable combination of thin and fair, and when paired with my exotic Muslim name, often get turned into an object of fascination or some kind of conquest. I have always been cushioned in the idea that I possess a prettiness, which has filled me with this particular dread because it meant that I was palatable to men, and also this irritation that this 'privilege' is something that they confer onto me.

It is for this very reason that I find myself unable to internalise the 'your hotness is your own' as a self-love mantra. If it weren't for the male-identified 'privileges' of being a hot girl, I would probably even forget that I had a body. The other thing, and this is a big one, is that I never really acted like how young pretty women are supposed to behave, and I don't mean this in a cute way. Without getting into the specifics of all the harassment and bullying I have experienced, I recognised very early on that that the thrill of being exceptionalised is followed by the violence and disposability of not being sanitised enough, of not being the kind of 'good girl' men want to protect.

There came a point at which being cast as the modern-day trophy girlfriend filled me with an icky restlessness. The more powerful men thought I was, the more disposable I knew I had become, because the condition of my desirability was that I always had to be exactly what they wanted me to be, and nothing else. The initial point of the thrill for me was never that I was 'not like other girls', it was that I was better than the boys. But this was just me being stupid and hopeful;

boys would never acknowledge this as fact, and the more threatened they feel, the crueller they become.

It is hard to discuss myself in this way as a retrospective, packing years of my life into this terse linearity, so I can find a way to make the present easier to talk about. The easiest way I can describe these convoluted modes of recognition is through this quote from a Hannah Black interview: 'I must be a woman because you treat me how you treat women.'

This is what it felt like, this acute powerlessness. While I can understand the feminine to be a source and expression of power, the truth is this is never how I experienced my girlhood. I began to feel the heartbreak of not being one of the boys, of not being hotter than the boys, of not being hot to the boys. A strange, shameful condition of being trapped between a 'fuck you!' and a 'pick me!' I find myself constantly reminding myself that I am not a *bechaari* because even that is something men want. Or I tell myself that a twenty-year-old girl worried about not being pretty is one of the least important, most common things in the world, except assuming the voice of a mean old man against my feelings don't make them go away.

The thing is: how do I have sex when I want to rupture everything men see as desirable about me—because I know by now that this catalogue of desirable girl types only exist to make you feel as small as possible, to slot you so they don't have to see you. How do I have sex when I don't even see anything desirable about me—because realising these things about how men see you can actually make you terrified of being seen at all.

A few months ago, my friends were describing the rush of wanting to fuck people they see passing by: their types, the fantasy, the urgency, the lewdness of it. I remember having nothing to say because I just didn't think anyone would reciprocate my desire to fuck. How do you even fantasise when you are unable to negotiate your own fuckability within yourself? How do you see other people as attractive when you don't think of yourself as someone anyone would be attracted to? How do you see other people when you can barely see yourself?

I was recently at a panel on 'Technology and Erotics,' and the India head of a popular global online dating app said that Indians in their twenties have already dated more than people in their forties. There is this narrative that us post-liberalisation babies have access to greater vocabularies of desire and have more avenues to operationalise that desire. The pressure to be having sex as proof of our desirability is now compounded with this strange '*Jab main tumhari age ki thi toh TV peh ek he channel aata tha: Doordarshan*' type of generational guilt. I remember laughing at what a perfect little sexless Indian girl I am, hidden like that black-and-white channel behind the frenetic technicolour.

Being suspended in sexlessness when all of your friends are constantly in relationships, between relationships or hooking up makes the holy trinity of sex positivity, body positivity and self-love feel like a consolation prize. My attempts at rejecting prettiness resulted in me desexualising myself. My desire to unravel the constituent parts of my desirability became a way for me to find different ways to tell myself that I am unattractive, and when you relate to yourself in this particular mode of self-hatred, you begin to see the different ways that social and personal interactions are structured to remind you of it.

I would stand by idly as men I was talking to would ask out a friend, often wondering why I never measured up or received that kind of attention. There are numerous permutations of this exact feeling, stretched across different circumstances, all amounting to the same thing: being in a perennial state of feeling rejected. The paranoia of being thought of as ugly and unfuckable, the most unladylike feeling.

I developed a fear of being seen and judged. I got used to panic attacks and crying uncontrollably in public. Every time I had to venture outside, I would have to spend hours emotionally training myself. On many days, I would be too scared to even step out of my room to use the bathroom. I had already fallen in unreciprocated love with someone, a desire that embedded me in a circular relationship between hope, longing and rejection. The question of whether I am pretty or not drains, corrodes and harms me so much that I would rather we didn't live in a world where these things mattered. I wish there was no such thing as prettiness, but this is an unrealistic hope. So, yes, I would rather be pretty than ugly, but don't tell anyone I said that because we're all beautiful, as you know.

How to deal with the dilemma of hotness as a feminist? In a journey to be your own person/woman? Either you commit yourself to being ugly as a statement or you think of everything about you as attractive, also as a statement. Desiring in spite of feeling undesirable. Desiring in spite of feeling like your ugliest, most unfuckable self. If there's one thing I have learnt, it is to listen to what my paranoias and fantasies are trying to tell me. Who do I tell myself I have to be in order for me to stop punishing myself? Whose pleasure, whose power? I have been using hetero-romance as a way to wound myself, oscillating between wanting to reject everything I have been told I should be and feeling rejected because I never was 'that girl' anyway.

I found some brief respite in the image of the exceptional girl, but then there is also the violence, the heartbreak and the anxiety of what will happen if it is revealed that I am not exceptional. I would like to derive no pleasure at all from how men see me because then I can get rid of the pain of not being a man. But it is hard to speak about detachments when there isn't exactly anything else you can attach yourself to.

Then there is the complexity of what I actually fantasise about, which is being loved in spite of heterosexuality and patriarchy. I want to exist outside the realm of dating, outside this thing of being judged for having a face and a body, outside of these ritualised prevarications.

I don't care how much sex you have and how soon. Often, critiques of dating turn into moralistic ventures and, like, I'm a chill and cool girl, I promise. I just want to figure out what desirability means and why I feel me being who I am renders me unfuckable. Perhaps, most importantly, I have learnt to not let rejection turn me into some stereotype of male dejection, to wrench it away from narratives of entitlement and abuse. Rejection is physically overpowering. The days you feel it, you are completely engulfed, and packed within is an urgency that needs direction.

I was terrified when I told a boy that I had feelings for him, that I was willing to commit to him. In the absence of the kind of reciprocation I had fantasised about, I turned into a figure of obsessive insecurity that did not respect his boundaries. There has to be a space to mediate all of this that is not retributive—you don't want to punish yourself or the other person.

I keep holding on to this kind of grace, which I think helps me, but I also wonder how anger can be restorative. I don't have the answers because I am figuring out the script for myself, which in itself is a feminist triumph. I want to believe, at least I think I do, that it will guide us towards loving ourselves with as much care and generosity as we extend to others in our daydreams.

Aliza Khan is a filmmaker based in Austin, USA, and an ex-intern of Agents of Ishq.

Of Simps, Sluts and My Time in a Boys' Club

Was being a 'cool girl' worth the self-hate?

NAYANA VACCHARAJANI

4 June 2021

I spent the two worst years of my life in a 'boys' club'. While correlation doesn't equal causation, which is to say that the boys' club wasn't necessarily the reason my life sucked, it seemed to symbolise all that sucked about it.

I had a hard time making friends throughout school. My parents and teachers said I shouldn't be so picky and I'd be lucky if people decided to accept me. It made me feel like I was a bad person who didn't deserve friends. This belief primed me for the conditioning, manipulation and internalised hate that I was about to be a part of.

Since I couldn't crack any of the all-girls social circles in high school, I asked my desk partner if I could sit with his group for lunch. He shrugged and said, 'Sure.' He didn't check with any of his friends or make a big deal about me being the only girl. I felt like I fit in, for the first time, just because they accepted, or should I say, *tolerated* me.

I knew nothing about rappers or fast cars or cricket, but it didn't matter. I was just happy to be included in something for the first time in fourteen years. The boys were also fascinated that I was not a 'girly girl' (whatever that meant), and they praised me for it. I got a kick out of their saying, 'She's a tomboy, *woh doosre ladkiyon ke jaise nahi hai.*' I began to associate all things girly with lameness or weakness. I rolled my eyes at those who left their long tresses open and wore Forever21 clothes. I gagged at girls who loved romantic comedies because, to quote Kartik Aaryan from *Pyaar ka Punchnama,* '*Saari ladkiya ek jaise hi hoti hai,* bro.' And I did not want to be '*saari ladkiyan*'.

I remember once, when going out for dinner with this group, one of the boys didn't really want me to come. My friend then said, 'Chill, she's not like other girls. She's a cool girl, no?' He turned, directing the question towards me, smiling warmly. I blushed in happiness and modesty despite how cringey the statement was. I thought he meant I was cool for being myself, but I didn't see that he and the other boys thought I was 'cool' because I was different from the 'girly girls' in our school. There was an implicit binary here—if you were not a 'girly girl' you were immediately classified as someone who is 'like a boy', so you were respected by the boys.

That basically meant 'feminine' equalled being walked all over (and objectified) and 'masculine' meant worthy of respect. The question of why this equation existed arose in my mind. Who decided who was worthy of respect and who wasn't? What did that say about 'respect' and who deserved it?

The boys in my group spent a sizable chunk of the lunch break making sexual jokes or objectifying and commenting on girls' appearances. And their standards were *harsh*. I remember them drooling over a girl they considered an absolute goddess just because she looked Caucasian (white skin, light brown hair and hazel eyes) and was extremely underweight. Their language was full of words like 'simp' and 'slut'.

I didn't know how to process the locker room talk because of how conscious it made me about my own looks. I was by no means skinny, I had dark brown skin, frizzy hair and thick-rimmed glasses. I began wondering where I would rank on their standards. Thoughts like, 'I have a nice ass, maybe I'm a six if I'm lucky' or 'My skin is too tan today, would they even want me there?' were running through my mind. I knew in the back of my mind that their comments were inappropriate, but I didn't want to be a 'nag' and I thought their behaviour was just them 'being boys'. Now I wonder, what's the definition of being a boy? What does it mean every time we say that boys will be boys?

If this were a movie, they would be good friends who would accept and love me regardless. But in real life, they'd rub salt in my wounds every time. I would get comments like, 'Abey, dark chocolate!' and 'Did you roll in mud today?' when I walked in after PT class. I was reminded over and over again that I was undateable, ugly and would likely die a virgin through how they objectified other girls and their constant comments on body and facial features. Being a 'cool tomboy' had an unwritten rule: I had to grin at their jokes even if I was hurt, or I would lose my status as a 'cool girl' and be lumped with the 'dumb, girly girls'. Their stupid standards became what I judged myself and other girls on. Consequently, I found myself assessing my female peers and even adult women by the same standards. I looked at the women around me and would constantly, compulsively judge and rate their looks while feeling bad about myself. And the one time I agreed when these boys commented that a girl was hot, they started calling me a 'dyke' and a 'fag'!

And OH MY GOD, the alpha male aspiration. It was always 'protein-protein-protein' and 'quads-forearms-delts'. Statements about how women were 'hoes' or 'thirsty gold-diggers' made me feel guilty to even be a woman. They'd make the dumbest of comments on masturbation too—they thought No Nut November would transform them into hyper-masculine Greek gods. Each conversation made me feel guiltier, weaker, sadder and worse about myself on the whole and *yet,* I stuck with them.

While I considered myself a feminist, I don't think I understood its nuances or thought of patriarchy as a power structure that did more than just oppress women. In hindsight, I also see that the boys were so anxious to be regarded as 'real men' in front of their male friends that making such comments made them feel more secure. They probably also felt that wealth defined them as men (even though they were still in school), which explains why they thought girls would only be attracted to them if they were rich. I didn't understand that patriarchy encouraged boys to hypocritically judge and objectify women while making men feel inadequate if they lacked money or muscles. Looking back, I'm sure my desire to be included and loved overrode not only my principles but also my instincts of self-preservation.

I'm lucky that things got better and our group evolved into a more courteous one so as to accommodate future girlfriends. Soon enough, I befriended my alpha male friend's girlfriend, Deepti (who didn't fit any of his 'standards' either) and realised his behaviour in front of other guys was a facade for him to feel secure. He behaved differently when surrounded by mostly boys because he was so anxious to perform masculinity. He brought Deepti over to eat lunch with us one day, and everyone was extremely sweet, kind and respectful to her in a way they never were with me or girls outside the group. In the process, I was also spared from their bullying and could laugh with them instead of being laughed at.

Deepti and I found out that we both liked to swim in our free time, and started to go on swim dates together. I would always feel insecure about wearing the skin-tight, sleeveless hip-length swimsuits because I did not like the idea of boys at the pool seeing how (in my words) 'pear-shaped' my body was, so I wore knee-length, loose swimsuits. When Deepti got out of the changing room, I saw her in exactly the kind of swimsuit I'd be afraid to wear at a public pool. She was far from thin. In fact, she was more 'pear-shaped' than I thought I was, and she nonchalantly, comfortably carried it. She didn't appear to be hunching her shoulders or sucking her waist in like I did when I thought I looked fat in my clothes. Inspired by her, I began wearing the tight, backless black swimsuits that I was saving for 'when I get thinner'. That was when I saw that no one really seemed to notice or care about how fat I was looking. In fact, I liked how it flattered my silhouette. I enjoyed our races to the deep end even more now that my swimsuit streamlined my posture.

We even gossiped about and laughed at the boys in our group. Like me, she also thought that Ashwin was an asshole, Arhan's life seemed to only revolve around food and porn, and Dev was a whiny brat. She scoffed at (and looked past) her boyfriend's machismo and hinted at him having a sweet, funny and charming personality, which was nice to hear after I had worried about how my generation of men would turn out. When I realised this possibility, I paid more attention to the times his soft interior shone through, and noticed that it happened more often than I thought.

This opened my mind to the possibility of forming a deeper bond with him. Maybe I could be his 'girl best friend' (yes, the cringe is strong with this one!). We did end up forming a more real, deep connection where he made me feel good about myself and we ended up bonding over art and memes. Who would've imagined?

When I turned sixteen, I changed schools. In the new school, I got to know a boy who seemed alpha male-ish at first glance, but cried openly, watched romcoms, questioned his conditioning (and is the coolest guy I know). I understood how fluid these things are, and how magical it can be to escape the stereotypes and assumptions about who we can be. I also saw that not all boys are by nature (or aspire to be) alpha males.

In conversations about new concepts we were learning, he was interested in the history of what is considered abnormal and normal. Sometimes, when talking about something that was sexist, I would brace myself for a rant on how feminists are actually 'misandrists', but that never happened and we had some really stimulating conversations. Around the same time, I watched a few videos on the 'not like other girls' phenomenon and realised it was happening to me. The pieces were falling into place.

My new friend struck me as laidback yet very absorbed in conversation, and extroverted but not overwhelmingly so. He radiated a subtle strength, not as in-your-face as my old friends but enough to let you know he was secure and powerful enough in his space to not encroach upon others' boundaries. I saw that it's possible to wear your feelings on your sleeve and make people laugh while also liking stereotypically 'male' things like football and sports cars. I finally understood what it meant to be secure in my femininity and, well, in my own self, and I am still exploring it by forming stronger female friendships and practising complimenting my fellow women rather than bringing them down. Nowadays, after a year of practising this, I finally feel more like my real self.

Nayana is a student of psychology and philosophy. She enjoys making art, doing yoga and wearing printed kurtis. She wrote this essay while interning at Agents of Ishq.

Why Men Don't Talk About Masturbators—and Other Questions You Never Thought to Ask

How restricting sex to peno-vaginal intercourse hinders possibilities of self-pleasure

ABHISHEK ANICCA

4 March 2021

At a work-related meeting, I opened my phone to check something, and an advertisement flashed on my phone—for a fleshlight, a male masturbator. In sheer panic, I pressed the phone so hard that it turned off. It was no surprise really that it appeared. I had been Googling fleshlights all night, trapped between deciding whether to invest three thousand rupees on a masturbator, or to rely on my good old hands to do the deed. Moreover, buying a cheap masturbator that was definitely Chinese *maal* might have been the start of a hilarious tragedy.

I have never heard men around me talk about masturbators. I asked some of my single male friends if they would give it a try, and they looked at me as if I had assaulted their masculinity. There is hardly anything more fragile than the Indian male ego, especially when talking about sex. Most straight men, in the heteronormative set-up, feel they are entitled to sex. And by extension, women.

My own position as a disabled, chronically ill person forces me to raise these uncomfortable questions because I know I am not entitled to anything, except maybe love and kindness. It also makes me search for new ways of finding pleasure through my body. The idea of sex within our hetero outlook is so rigid, that anything other than peno-vaginal missionary is considered out of syllabus. This orthodoxy has led to many of my possible relationships ending even before they begin.

This one time, I had a urinary tract infection (my Achilles heel) in the middle of a short (and rare) affair that I was involved in. For an able-bodied man, this would have been no big deal. But because of my chronic illness, everything stops working when I am ill. Complete *chakka* jam. I searched for ways to make it work. A penis extender for three grand; would it work? How should I talk about it? Unfortunately, I couldn't make that decision on time and that affair had to end, somewhat prematurely.

Explaining my body before getting into any sort of relationship, long or short, can be embarrassing. It shouldn't be, ideally, but it is. It turns into a booklet of things I can't do. And before I have finished reading out the booklet, my potential partner has moved on. My claim to being a man is often judged by the standards of how an able-bodied, straight man is supposed to be, in body and behaviour. No matter what most folks claim, men and women in heteronormative settings are still attracted to typical (sometimes caricature-ish) masculine and feminine traits.

When you are disabled, expressing yourself sexually can be difficult. A friend of mine who is quadriplegic told me of his struggles with pleasuring himself. I was stumped. I hadn't even thought about it before. Giving yourself pleasure suddenly seemed like a privilege. It shouldn't be. There should be tools to help severely disabled individuals. We need sex therapists. We need counselling. There is so much to do, and yet, I don't see activists talking about it. It's not easy for most disabled people to tell these stories. Most of them live with their families, who are their primary caretakers. Talking about sex can be a process full of shame and embarrassment. Disability is supposed to be about survival, not desire, apparently.

All of this takes me back to one thing—the idea of male self-pleasure. Why don't we talk more about it? Is it because of the inherent nature of patriarchy where men are always entitled to sex? Or is it the dominant idea of masculinity which sees men in a certain way—'Everything is working, right?' It might be a combination of both these factors. It's no surprise that even for able-bodied men, going to a sexologist is taboo. It's on such taboos that most quacks run their businesses, spray-painting men's problems onto city walls: 'Reach out to your nearest baba or dawakhana.'

We live in a society where the idea of women pleasuring themselves has been sexualised. It is used as titillating imagery—fine when men talk about it, but when women actually do it, everyone gets jittery. As for men, they can joke about sex and masturbation, but can't actually talk about it, about doing it, about enjoying it. The heteronormative sexism embedded at the core of what is considered 'masculine' sexuality dictates what kind of pleasure is acceptable and what isn't. In such a setting, finding pleasure, or even talking about it, is regimented by the rules of society.

It's not just about disability. Self-pleasure is an inherent aspect of one's sexuality, something that needs to be spoken about and encouraged. It can help in developing different perspectives about pleasure amongst men—as individuals who experience pleasure, and not simply take it from others to prove their masculinity. These conversations can contribute to awareness about diverse bodies, something that is the need of the hour. Instead of teaching them to draw maps of conquest, men should be taught to openly embrace their bodies. This will surely help them learn to embrace other bodies, boost their own emotional and psychological wellbeing, ease the shame and violence around sex, make consent understandable, even automatic, and make this world a better place.

The so-called 'normal' that heteronormativity loves to categorise people as disables everyone sexually in some way, and those with disability even more.

Personally, I feel a conversation about self-pleasure could do wonders for men with disabilities. In a world where marriage is the primary gateway to sexual fulfilment, yet full of rejection and unrequited love, finding ways to love themselves and their bodies will definitely improve self-image and bring them confidence to be successful in future relationships and life.

Plus, we will have hilarious stories of men's junk getting stuck in Chinese-made masturbators.

Abhishek Anicca is a writer, poet and researcher. He identifies as a person with disability and chronic illness, which shapes his creative and academic endeavours.

As a Man, am I Condemned to Choose Violence Over Love? Maybe Not

I hit her. The realisation of what I did and the guilt it brought is unbearable even now

PAWAN HANS BADWAL

15 October 2019

It was just a normal conversation. Meenu,* a dear friend—and maybe a little more than a friend—was upset and sharing some problems she was having at work. I tried listening to her and calming her down, but it wasn't helping. And the frustration and stress—of my own unfinished work, and my agitation at not being able to calm her down—grew. Even though the cause for my panic seems so trivial to me now, the rush of emotions that I felt at the time was enormous. And not knowing how to cope with it, I did something horrendous.

I hit her.

The realisation of what I did, and the guilt it brought is unbearable even now. How had I been able to make that transition from hugging and expressing affection to being violent with her so easily? Searching for answers to this drew me back, to memories of being younger and witnessing beatings at home and learning to hit as a matter of course.

Is that what shaped my ideas about touch? Then why did it seem at times like such an unsatisfactory explanation for what I did—that is, if there could be an explanation that wasn't an excuse?

Touch is, in many ways, fundamental to how we communicate—whether it is fear, love, authority, affection or even just a sense of comfort—and it plays a big role in how we build relationships with people. Does what we learn about touch as children shape our relationship with it as adults? I decided to dig into my own memories, and speak to a few other people about theirs, to find out.

―

When you think about touch within families, do you think of it as being comforting? Do hugs and caresses come to mind?

They certainly do for me. My parents were sometimes affectionate with me as a child. At the same time, I would often see my brother being beaten excessively by my parents for small mistakes that were more often than not blown out of proportion in their heads. It would upset me.

Even so, I had internalised the fact that hitting someone was a natural and acceptable response. I had also been told, 'What kind of brother are you if you don't keep your younger brother in control?' Looking back, I can clearly see how my behaviour changed towards my brother. From initially opposing my parents' mistreatment of him, to hitting him myself when he was not able to understand a maths problem even after repeated explanations, my actions had shifted even though on some level I knew what I was doing was not correct. I don't think I can ever justify my aggression, but sometimes I felt like I had no choice. It was expected of me. And it was how I learnt to express frustration and try to gain control of a situation.

I know of other people, college students like me, for whom violence was a large part of childhood. Abhijit, a twenty-one-year-old communications student, tells me he had been beaten a lot by his father, and used to feel aggression and hatred towards him. Gita, a twenty-one-year-old student of fashion design, also has a fractured relationship with her parents. The youngest of three siblings, she would see her brother and sister being beaten as punishment—though she never experienced it herself. However, she says that a consequence of witnessing this has been that she is not close to her parents, that she has severed ties to her father and, to a certain extent, with her mother.

My own parents' actions seemed too harsh to me and I didn't understand why it had to be so. I'm sure every family has its way of scolding and disciplining children, but my family's way affected me quite a lot. I knew that their abuse—and my own participation in it—was wrong. But I still did it … and that left me very confused and anguished for a long time. I too had a rocky relationship with my parents growing up.

In the cases of Abhijit, Gita and I, our parents probably did what they thought was best for their children. All the same, even though not all of us were beaten by them directly, and violence wasn't our only experience of childhood, simply witnessing their violence as we grew up damaged our relationships with them. That was perhaps the opposite of what our parents intended, but it was a sad reality for us, at least while we were young. The shortage of a loving touch created a rift in our families that hasn't fully healed.

But feeling the absence of loving touch from one's family isn't only for those of us who grew up with beatings. Radhika,* twenty-two, pursuing an MA, lost her parents when she was very young. She lives with her guardians, whom she calls her father and mother. Although she has been living with them for quite some time, and they do care for her, the element of touch—that experience of someone affectionately running their fingers through your hair or a warm tight hug—was missing.

She feels she didn't have the privilege of experiencing the affection one gets from one's parents while growing up. And so, she is keen to experience it. She talks about how important touch and affection is in one's childhood, and how the absence of it has taught her to value it more. Radhika also tells me about how an older man touched her inappropriately when she was a child. Though at that age she was not aware about 'good touch' and 'bad touch', she knew that she was uncomfortable with it. Even though it remains an unpleasant memory, it hasn't made her averse to being touched; rather, it has increased her desire for a more caring, warm, affectionate touch.

Does coming from a loving home where the only kind of touch you've experienced involves hugs and caresses automatically mean having a healthy sense of touch as a grown up? I have wondered about this sometimes. Meenu, who had just turned twenty-one, and was in her final year of studying journalism, comes from a stable, happy family. (When I asked her about her family, she told me something that made me feel more guilt and pain for the way I treated her: 'There has never really been any violence in my household, and so I'm not used to it. I am used to being treated very nicely.') Meenu has always been comfortable with experiencing and expressing physical affection to her mother and other women in the house. She is more reserved with the male members of her family, but the love remains. Going to college has put her in situations where it is more common to touch others and be touched—bonding with friends by hugging, putting an arm around someone, pulling and pushing them playfully. And she feels that in all these situations she has been able to be a stable, open person, who knows as well as firmly asserts her boundaries in a healthy way. To me, she is one example of how when parents are loving and gentle, their children grow up to be confident and comfortable with themselves. My close friend Neelima,* a twenty-two-year-old communications student, also says she had 'a lovely childhood' and grew up with a healthy sense of touch. I have known her for four years as a happy-go-lucky, very physically affectionate person. So you will understand my surprise when she told me that she feels awkward about being touched, and is actually not fine with physical contact, except when it comes to people she is really close to. On some level, she knows that she appears affectionate because she is a people-pleaser—she says and does things that she thinks people would like, at the cost of how she herself might really feel. She is afraid of losing her near and dear ones—an insecurity of hers, and I wonder sometimes if her showing tremendous affection to people close to her might be a function of this insecurity.

At any rate, Neelima reminds me that in my search to find a link between touch in childhood, our relationships with our families and touch in adulthood, there are no absolutes, no finalities. If having a happy childhood doesn't necessarily guarantee that you have a healthy sense of touch as a grown-up, and you may still have to work on it, might it mean that growing up with an unhealthy sense of touch doesn't necessarily mean that that's how it must always be?

Speaking to different people about their early years has made me realise that for many of us, adolescence was a tough time. My formative years left me with scars that are yet to heal and issues with low self-esteem, that spilled over into my relationships with other people—and perhaps this is the case for others as well. Some of us, as a friend of mine puts it, have been victims of victims, growing up with our parents' violence. And whether we know it or not, we often absorb these behaviours. I see people around me who mirror their parents' opinions and actions, and I know it's the same for me too.

But in diving back into my childhood looking for answers to the question of why I hit Meenu, my aim hasn't been to dump blame for my actions on my parents, or to claim that that's the only way I know how to be. With time, things have changed. I have cried before them, spoken to them about everything I had felt, and they too have responded with introspection and compassion. I understand now the intent behind their actions—they wanted to make sure my brother and I did everything right, to keep us safe from society's comments and disapproval—though I do think there were better ways of expressing that concern. They could have let us know why they were disciplining us, and reassured us that we were still loved. I was never sure of their love growing up. And unlike the director of the film *Kabir Singh*, Sandeep Reddy Vanga, I don't see violence as an expression of love. Sometimes we forget where love ends and possessiveness begins, and I think violence is a form of that possessiveness, used to control others.

I felt traumatised by the violence in my childhood, but I think I need to move beyond it—others have before me.

Abhijit says his relationship with his parents got better as he grew older and they disciplined him less. Gita says that even though she felt very affected by the violence she witnessed in her childhood, with time, she has started being at peace with herself, and says that whatever she had witnessed shaped the way she is today—silent, stoic and composed. She tells me that when she found herself battling with issues, she attended a four-day yoga session that allowed her to examine her actions and emotions, helped her deal with her problems and helped her be a better person. Though she may not have reached a place of healing by working through her problems with her family, she was able to take the initiative to find it outside of her family—something I deeply admire her for, and hope to learn myself.

I feel cheered by the fact that Gita's experiences don't appear to have affected how she experiences touch as an adult. At first glance, she does not seem like someone who likes hugs. But if you are really dear to her, she becomes a hugger, constantly showering you with affection. She likes to let people know even when she feels a tinge of affection for them: she'll tell them, act it out or leave notes for her loved ones that make them feel good.

Funnily, if she had to be a parent, she says she would be, 'A contradictory one. One who is very loving and caring, but is ready to hit and scold the child to make sure that things are done the way they ought to be.'

And the more I think about my own parents and my childhood, I realise that violence hasn't been their only legacy.

Have you ever taken a step back to think about how you behave with children around you? Personally, I have mostly replicated the mannerisms and habits that I have seen in my mother. The words that she uses, and the way she plays with them, are now mine. Other friends tell me they've noticed this in themselves too.

I also think that the way I go about romance is something I learnt from my parents. I have often found myself imagining scenarios in which I am expressing my love to the significant one in my life in the ways I have seen my father do so for my mother—teasing her, random kisses, romantic nicknames and so on. Literature and other media might have had a little influence on my notion of romance, but most of it comes from what I saw between my parents and grandparents. I guess I mirror my parents' actions in more ways than I realise.

And speaking with Shivam, twenty-two, my hostel roommate, made me realise a beautiful thing—my parents have taught me the importance of being sensitive and considerate of others. To think about how someone might feel or get affected by my actions and words.

Moving forward, we all in some way know what's right or wrong, and I'll try to stick to that. And when I have children of my own, and have to deal with the pressure of caring for, protecting and nurturing a whole human being, I hope I am more willing to tailor my actions to be supportive of my children, to employ methods that are more encouraging towards better behaviour than disciplining bad behaviour. To be more open and willing to accept their mistakes, as well as mine and those of my partner, friends and family. After all, we're all in the continuous process of learning.

And from Meenu, who has given me the gift of forgiveness, I've learnt that I have to let the past go and strive to be better. She has taught me calmness and compassion, that there are other ways of dealing with stress and conflict that don't involve lashing out. And she's shown me that the person I want to be from now on depends not on my parents, or my childhood, but on me.

Pawan is a visual designer. He wrote this essay during an internship with Agents of Ishq.

From Lost and Found Poems of a Girl Who Liked Sex

NISHA SUSAN

Ahem

Smart women,
My grandmother says,
Smart women
can hold their men
in the palm of their hands.
I'm beginning to wonder
what exactly
She's talking about.

A Fish Dinner

Some boy
Sunk his head
Between her thighs
And said you smell of the sea.
She liked his style
And let him swim.
A decade later
On a beach she still looks smug.

Nisha Susan is a writer and editor. She is the co-founder of the feminist online magazine The Ladies Finger and the award-winning indie media organisation Grist Media.

A PLACE IN BETWEEN

I Believe in the Promises Made by Passing Strangers
Cruising and the City

Leaving behind the threshold of our homes, what other boundaries do we cross?

ANINDYA SHANKAR DAS

23 July 2019

As a child, there were few places I feared more than a public toilet.

The way they smelt of men, the way that no amount of phenyl or naphthalene could mask the rankness of ammonia, was in such contrast to the tiny, cool bathroom at home that smelt of Lifebuoy soap and Sunsilk shampoo. Ma would always bang suspiciously on the door if I spent longer than five minutes inside.

But behind the terror was also a nervous excitement. I had no idea I was also attracted to men back then in junior school (or did I?), but I did know that there was a whole code in those pheromones which stirred something forbidden. 'Say no, say no,' an insistent voice whined, and I said no to public toilets and blamed it on hygiene.

Till that one evening in Pune.

As a student in Pune, on an evening walk after a particularly long film in a particularly cold theatre, I had to break the old, personal taboo and use a public restroom. It just so happened that the one that I was destined to use that night was right out of my worst nightmares. Dark in a way that made me wonder about mugging even as I struggled to hold it in, and putrid in a way that I could smell from across the street. I walked into the darkness and unzipped. In that moment, as what felt like twenty years of piss flooded out of me, I was awash with gratefulness for the existence of every public toilet ever. I will never forget the streetlight streaming through a broken window into that ruin of a toilet. God does speak in mysterious ways.

And then, as I adjusted to the light, I saw a grotesque shape to my right, in the shadows. It had four hands and a writhing body. It was my monster, my curse let loose. I froze.

The next moment defined my immediate life to come; the monster uncoiled itself into two young men. My entry had interrupted them, but when they understood I was harmless, the kissing slowly resumed (as I realised that the only monster that existed was in my head). I stood at my urinal, transfixed in terror. And excitement.

Later, I stammered mentally, briskly walking down the footpath, flushed with fear and desire, unable to shake away the image of the two men. Something unleashed in that toilet, something that I had bottled up for twenty years in societally imposed in-sanitation.

From there, my fascination with cruising began. I had read a little on online forums about cruising in my teens (mostly with disgust), but now I would take long walks across Pune in the dead of the night—walks that mostly led to the extremely cruisy railway station toilet. It was big, that loo, and manned by a shrewd-looking fellow who seemed to be measuring the world in the way he chewed his gutkha.

The moment you entered, there was a huge stained mirror that looked on as all kinds of men washed faces and limbs. Taking a right would get you into an L-shaped hall with a high ceiling, where an incessant stream of travellers attended to nature's call. None of them really bothered to take the trouble to walk down to the end of the L—and that is where I learnt to head; a place where a different sort of call, no less urgent, was being attended to.

Often, I would stand at the far end of that railway station loo, pretending to pee as if my life depended on it, cheeks flushed red, as around me strangers looked into each other's eyes, and depending on a nod or a nay, changed the pissoirs they were standing at. Men unzipped and tugged at themselves as strangers with silent, gentle hands helped. Depending on the time of the night, more would happen. Never was a word spoken.

At twenty, I vehemently believed that sex was possible only when in love. That the craving of my body was a test against being tainted. Never mind that I wound up at the toilet so often; when someone would reach out, I would shy away and leave immediately, burning with shame.

One night at around 2 a.m., I saw someone I really liked. He was like me—nervous, naïve, young and a little sleepy. His eyes darted to mine as mine did to his. He took off the handkerchief hiding his face, a dark sweaty face with a curly beard, and adjusted the heavy bag on his back. I took a deep breath and made my way next to him. After an eternity, we touched.

I forgot the smell of piss, the leaking pipe, the footsteps around me. I was completely in my body. In that moment, in the most public of private spaces, I finally saw the visible in the invisible. I had found the end of one road. Or perhaps its beginning.

I smiled at the toilet attendant as I left that night. He was a little taken aback.

Slowly, in the act of making eye contact with strangers and learning to read body language, I began to see how my community had subverted urban public spaces. And I began to talk to the people I met about their experiences of cruising.

At 5.30 p.m., Palash leaves office as usual after a long, sweaty day of work. An affable *bhadrolok* a year away from retirement, he says a polite goodbye to his colleagues. Putting distance between himself and them, Palash walks off the road that leads to the metro station and takes a detour.

Just a block away from Dalhousie, a bustling business district in Kolkata, is an old public toilet adjacent to a mostly empty park. The ancient toilet attendant outside gives him a customary nod—Palash has been visiting this loo once or twice a week for the last thirty-odd years.

'As someone in my fifties now, I never could "come out" the way people do today, though I've known I'm attracted to men my whole life. In the early 1980s, one day, soon after starting work, I was talking to a man at a bus stop. He took me to this toilet which I had crossed but never entered. Inside was another world. Two men were kissing and people were peeping over the cubicles at each other. I left that day but ended up returning—it became a haven for me after work, a small break that let me be myself before I caught the bus back to my wife and child. It took time, but I grew confidant enough to make eye contact with men and take them to the park nearby. And now, although so much has changed, I can't stop going back there once in a while,' says Palash as we sit talking on a roadside bench, drinking chai.

I know what it feels like—it seems so much like my own story, except instead of a family, I would go back to a jolly group of friends at the hostel. Friends to whom I was out— but being out doesn't really take care of desire, does it? Desire sometimes pulls you down its own rickety road, scented with pheromones and carpeted in shadows. Millennia of bodily desire carving a path through memory and morality, through concrete and contact. A path that leads to parks, toilets, cinema halls, bars, massage parlours and stations—places to pick up strangers or maybe just have a go right there. The deity of desire is not one to always take it lying down. The spirit of sex resides as much in spaces as it does in human bodies. Think of cruising as a pilgrimage.

Before I encountered the world of offline cruising, meeting men meant hanging around in Internet chatrooms or on sites dedicated to queer men dating (yes, it took years before the straight community caught up). No one really had profile pictures in those days, and come to think of it, wandering about in a Yahoo chatroom with bradpittt2002 or myztikaldude007 was like cruising in a park, only with blindfolds on. Words became the primary connect. Then came a blurry photo.

On the other hand, cruising revealed a language older than words, flowing through blood and bone and brain. Not just fingertips on a keyboard but an entire body moved to the rhythm of the immediate environment, saying what was needed to be said and hiding what needed to be hidden. A body that dared to say—I need more than a computer. A body that dared to follow the shadow between choice and compulsion.

If not for cruising spaces, where else would so many members of the queer community, many living in the closet and distanced from a 'gay' identity, find sexual release? Many with no privacy at home. Many without a conventional home. (Surprising as it may be to some younger readers, many people in India don't have access to the Internet, let alone smartphones.)

When 'old-timers' like Palash talk, it reveals not just the thrill of cruising but also the diversity within the queer community. They speak of how class, caste, language and body types would not be as segregated as they are now on apps with all their filters and raging body trends. Often profiles proudly advertise—only English, no femmes, no dark, no Asians, no fat, no uncles. No this, no that. A far cry from a scenario where a civil servant would be standing beside a daily wage labourer in a park while a student checked both of them out from a distance.

Rejection has always been a part of cruising, but that rejection is at least a conscious one—momentarily bittersweet, tangible. Like smartphones themselves, their users are subject to the copy-paste virus, leaving something as powerful as rejection to the vagaries of consumerism.

Those born into smartphones might view cruising as a desperate act, sometimes forgetting that public spaces could be safer and more measured than, or at least as risky as, inviting a complete stranger into one's bedroom. There is a growing restlessness, a feeling that app-driven dating/hooking up forces people to be less authentic versions of themselves. So many of my friends are fed up of Grindr or Tinder—an endless cycle of deleting and reinstalling. Drowning the user in a deluge of profiles, all the app seeks is your attention; a desire that belongs to a lover is devoted to an algorithm. A body, made up of so many things, is reduced to an identity.

While cruising, the 'feeling' of another person matters when it comes to attraction and safety. And it matters a lot. What really is anonymity? Does a profile photo held in your palm make the person more known than a stranger you have been exchanging glances with on a train? Your body senses things it needs to know.

As Pankaj, a gay transman living in Mumbai, said to me, 'I prefer cruising because I can feel the vibe of another human in the way that I never can in a photograph or a few words. You can communicate everything through your eyes. Body language really means a lot to me. I get attracted to different kinds of men when I am out there. Maybe if I saw those same people on a profile, I wouldn't feel the same.'

Pankaj says he has quit online dating and chooses to meet his partners through cruising. I ask him if cruising spots are still active in Mumbai. He gives me a wide, naughty smile. 'You know all those romantic songs about when eyes meet across a crowded place? *Jaane kya tune kahi! Jaane kya maine suni! Baat kuch ban he gayi* ... (Who knows what you said, who knows what I heard, things came together anyway ...). That's it really, isn't it? Eyes are meeting all around you, constantly, and sometimes magic happens.'

Karim drives an autorickshaw in Bangalore. In his early twenties, he hails from a village in Uttar Pradesh and tells me he has never heard of any of the dating apps—Grindr, PR (Planet Romeo) or Tinder. The only gay pages he knows are on Facebook but he has never used them as he doesn't have a smartphone yet. He wants one though so that he can use GPS.

How then does he manage to meet men? Shyly, he tells me that there are men all around if you only know how to look.

'The eyes are most important. And touch. You can tell by touch. A few casual words maybe. But the eyes are the most important. Once in a while, I will catch a passenger staring at me. But I never do anything during business time!'

I ask him if he is aware that cruising can be a source of STIs due to risky, unsafe sex. 'Yes,' he says, 'though I have not always been careful in the past. When I first came to the city, I did not even know of STIs. Now I do. I plan to have a blood test soon.

'Check out that man standing across the street. Look at the way he has been staring at us the whole time. Wanna go say hi?' jokes Karim.

In my opinion, the queer community has a curious way of both taking stock of disease and ignoring it. Most cruising spaces rarely see hardcore sex happen. Most of the activity is 'soft'. Yet, with PrEP available to those with money, where do the rest of us stand vis-à-vis unsafe sex in a world that has overcome a certain amount of paranoia around HIV? And, of course, HIV is just one of many STIs to affect people.

Whether it is through cruising or through apps, there is definitely a risk of STIs associated with quick, anonymous sex with multiple partners. Incidentally, once upon a time, a toilet in a popular park in Pune was so known for men having sex with men inside that there was a condom vending machine installed beside the sink. Tellingly, it was dismantled a few years ago, reflecting our state's contentious understanding of sexual health and desire, despite other progressive changes in laws.

Especially before Section 377 was read down, plainclothes policemen or local hoodlums in search of a quick buck routinely pretended to be looking for sex in known cruising spots and then robbed and physically or sexually assaulted their victims, often older gay men and transwomen. Sometimes, this extortion continued through blackmail for months or years. Surprisingly, these same policemen would have no qualms about waiting for a considerable time, often fully erect, at a urinal or a park bench. Perhaps they were pretending to themselves about other things too.

A student, R, who spoke to me was so shaken by their experience of being caught and harassed by the Delhi police in a public park two years ago that they still have nightmares about the incident. The beating. The threat of calling home. Taking every last paisa of a few thousand withdrawn for college admission. The humiliation by torchlight in a dark ground. They have not dared to go cruising again.

Thankfully, the story does have a happy ending. Noticing the visible distress, that night R's flatmate asked if anything was wrong. R broke down and spoke of their ordeal. In response, the flatmate came out of the closet. They fell in love and are still together.

～

Arnab shifted to Kolkata from a small town in West Bengal to pursue a college diploma. At over six feet tall, he is an imposing figure. Yet, he tells me that in his second visit to a soft porn theatre with a balcony famed for encounters that would put the screen to shame, he was almost forced into a sexual act by someone stronger than him.

'I had hardly ever even met anyone who is gay before. In my town, the nearest match on Grindr is a hundred and fifty kilometres away! And even though that guy tried to force me, I held my ground, and people around made him leave me alone. I dealt with it.

'I returned because this space felt like I belonged here, amidst these men. I feel lonely in the hostel. I feel like myself here. I feel like I will meet someone.'

Arnab is still a visitor to the hall, though much more confident and intimidating himself after a year of being a regular.

Consent in cruising is tricky. Without consent, cruising is not possible in public spaces.

How does one respond to a look in a tea stall? Or a gentle touch on the elbow in a train? Do they stop to ask for the time even though they are clearly carrying a phone? Is a smile returned? Or a lighter? These little things can go a long way in safely approaching a partner in a sea of people with different sexualities. It is part of the thrill—being right sometimes, being wrong at others. But cross the hazy line and cruising can become something else entirely. Something ugly. It is in either very crowded places like local trains or queer-dominated spaces, like the cinema balcony mentioned earlier, where consent becomes unimportant for some. Like most humans, many in the queer community too have a lot to understand about yes, no and maybe.

∽

Some of the most visible members of a cruising space, and often with exclusive spots of their own are members of the trans* community, mostly transwomen. They have been trailblazers in claiming and defending queer public spaces, many a time being at a much greater risk of violence. NGOs and trans individuals have filed a number of ongoing cases of extortion, physical and sexual abuse against perpetrators of violence in public spaces but a huge number of cases go unreported.

Sujatha, a transwoman from Chennai, says, 'Many of the members of our community are from working classes with no access to dating apps. They are definitely not comfortable with English. For them, cruising is not just a thrill or kink … it is the only way to meet partners.'

And lesbian/bisexual women are almost invisible when it comes to cruising in India. Tales of meeting strangers in bars, sport centres, malls, nightclubs or other spaces are common but there are hardly any specific cruising spaces for lesbians the way they are for gay men.

But in spite of this love persists, for cruising is not only about sex. Leaving behind the threshold of our homes, what other boundaries do we cross? Why is there an urge to risk it all for a seemingly anonymous encounter? At the heart of this dance is belonging. Of belonging to a community, to a moment, maybe even to another being. I have seen strangers touch each other like old lovers, I have met couples who have lived their entire lives together after a smile exchanged on a park bench.

~

There is no real way of classifying or simplifying the phenomenon of cruising. As cities change and policing becomes stronger and tech-based, old, much-loved cruising spots die and new ones take their place.

Is there a space for private queer love at home? Are all queer people supposed to leave their families or come out forcibly? Some of the most open expanses available to people are and will be public spaces. And they will always be used for the full spectrum of human expression.

As the smartphone market grows and the world becomes even more technologically controlled, it will be interesting to see the new turns that offline cruising takes. The primal drive to seek out partners that is such a basic foundation of us as humans will be impossible to wipe out, as much as any agency tries. We now live in a world where queer folk who grew up without the Internet live with those who have never been without it. Information is passed on forums, through films and articles. Many straddle both the worlds of offline and online cruising.

Young queer people (even with smartphones) now seek out cruising spots, and search for the history of their community. There is a power in these meetings, an ode to a spirit of community. As important as pride, as necessary as reading down Section 377.

The search for our true sexual selves is an elusive one, existing in some unclassifiable, intangible space that apps and matrimonials can't get to, that we ourselves spend a lifetime seeking to understand.

As far as I am concerned, the search has always led me to push a little outside my boundaries of class, language, geography, identity. For where does home, or even my body, begin ... and end? Why should I be conditioned into whom to like? Or where? I believe in the promises made by passing strangers.

Falling asleep in a train, watching crows squabble in a park, holding my nose as I cross a garbage vat, wolfing down street food that I know will punish me soon, weaving through a market and soaking it all in a quiet bar. For me, cruising is all this and more. Lights and locks. Love and looking.

As we finish our chai, Palash sums up what cruising is for him. And indeed for so many of us in cities, suburbs and towns, packed into our boxed lives in a society that is far from accepting of sexuality in general and queer sexuality in particular. 'Desire and loneliness,' he smiles as he gets up, glancing at his watch. 'Achha, I'll leave now. I have to get back home to my family.'

I decided to stay back.

After all, the cruising spot that Palash mentioned was right around the corner.

Anindya Shankar Das is an independent filmmaker, writer, chef and bodywork practitioner based in Bombay and Goa. They are always open to interesting work or collaborations.

More Than an Identity
How I Realised My Struggle was with Being Sexual, Not Homosexual

My identity as a queer person became a bit of a shield from the world of love, the world of sex

DEBASMITA DAS

11 June 2019

It is little-known among those in my circle that I serially crushed on boys (one per year) up to eighth grade. Maybe it's because after the last boy, I realised I was queer. And when you're queer, your story always begins from the moment you knew you were gay. From the moment you identified yourself as something different. As someone whose ability to desire and love required a label to be explained to everyone else. What was my sexuality before I knew? I don't know—and it seems no one is really curious.

I knew I was queer at different points in my life with different degrees of clarity. In eighth grade, when my heart did a somersault instead of the usual *dhadko-fying* when my Woman-Crush-Wednesday friend I was obsessed with sent me a text saying, 'I wish you were here,' I was aware I was at 10 per cent KIWG (Knew I Was Gay). When I Googled 'bisexual' and thought, 'Whoa, I can *love* love my friend?' I was at 20 per cent (but in denial) KIWG. When in twelfth grade, a girl told me she was a lesbian and I, ahem, promptly fell for her—I peaked at a 90 per cent *shit-ye-toh-real-ho-gaya* KIWG.

Thing is, I knew about LGBT rights and considered myself an ally very early. Before I even knew I was queer, I knew the term, the movement for their rights, the language of identity politics. I was already a feminist, and when people called my best friend 'corrupt' (a word used generously in middle school) for having too many friends who were boys, I could call it 'slut-shaming'. It was that time in my life when these words for experiences felt like they were liberating me. So when I finally knew I was gay, was I happy to have an identity that held some socio-political significance? A little, I guess. It did make me feel a bit like a *krantikari*. But soon I just got really, really confused.

Was I bisexual? But I hadn't liked guys for years by then. Was I *gasp* a homoromantic heterosexual? I seemed to fall in love with women more than lust after them. Lesbian? But what about that dirty history of light-eyed boys I had crushes on? Who'd believe me if I said I was lesbian? This yo-yoing between labels stopped only when I realised I could call myself queer and leave it at that. And yet, the search for that perfect word never really stopped.

Many labels have knocked at my door ever since. Genderfluid. Asexual. Demisexual. Anorgasmic. Sensual-sexual (my invention). 'Lesbian' pays a monthly visit, I swear. And in moments of sheer terror, 'Actually Straight (You're Just Faking It)' comes to says hi. For a year or so before I entered college, every second thought was about this, occupying my mental space much more than I'd expected. I thought I was obsessed. In that time somewhere in that relentless negotiation of determining who I was, I left behind my ability to fall in love or desire without the baggage of my queer identity. I pretend that the era of liking boys is irrelevant but perhaps it was the only time my sexuality was really just mine. Not a part of a larger discourse. Not different. Not relevant to anything or anyone but myself.

When I went to college, I was starting to know who I was. Although if I have to phrase it more honestly, I was starting to get better at explaining what I identified as. I started coming out to people and found solace in making queer art that further cemented me in people's eyes as That Queer Person. My work really was my refuge. While I was falling in love with close friends who were straight, roommates, beautiful seniors (basically everyone, the emotional ho that I was), I'd try to find answers through my work. When I was confused about why I sucked at understanding romance or approaching it, I analysed my queerness to death, and I made an animation that explained how heterosexuals had unlimited media to guide them in their love life, but us queers had nothing to teach us. When I was heartbroken and no politics could explain it, I would draw, and dump it on my Instagram. I'm still mentioned in some articles as a queer Insta artist (I call myself gay Rupi Kaur in private).

My personal would always be political. So I made a portfolio out of it. I was building a reputation as That Queer Person, as That Queer Artist. Among my friends, I was That Relentlessly Gay Friend. In truth, just as a person, I had no clue how to navigate my love and sex life. I had placed all my value in making my identity useful—in changing the world, in articulating a politics, and I always prioritised it over (or perhaps even interchanged it with) my actual personal life. I was out and proud, but inside I found myself unexpectedly stumbling upon shame more and more. That shame, though, was not about being queer.

The better half of every 'it gets better' narrative starts with coming out. I had already done that. I already knew that liking, loving, desiring women was okay. But my personal life still felt ... deeply sad. Whenever I fell for someone, the impossibility of it all would fall like a great weight on me. I was afraid of falling in love, because every time the person was either straight or not interested in me. I taught myself to confess my feelings but only did it when I was already in too deep. I didn't know how to flirt or test the waters with someone because I was at a stage where just the prospect of befriending a queer person itself would freak me out, forget expressing romantic or sexual interest in them. In college, we were surrounded by romancing and sex and hormones flying around. But I felt completely in the dark about how sexual interactions happened, let alone know how to engage in them myself.

I think I was never able to spot a queer person and just befriend them because somewhere I had convinced myself that if I was in a supportive environment, who was I to ask for more? I felt silly for wanting a community, wanting to seek out more queer people, for being single and utterly inexperienced in my personal life in spite of being in a liberal art school where, according to other Bangaloreans, 'every second person is bisexual'. If there was a word for cruising for queer women, I would have sucked at it. Whenever I went to queer events, the utter confidence with which people oozed sexuality or openly flirted with each other only served to reinforce my insecurities because I just didn't know how to get there. I was ashamed of struggling with my sexuality long after having done the entire 'I'm out and proud' thing. I guess what I didn't realise was that more than anything else, I was struggling with being sexual, not homosexual. This may not be different from anyone else, but for a queer person, when that struggle is reduced to 'coming out' or 'being accepted', and personal goalposts are all about resisting prejudice, it leaves out a big part of 'love learning'—of learning to love, to desire, and having a love and sex life.

I used to try to find the answers to all my struggles in my queerness, and to some extent, it did help to be reassured that, yes, it was more difficult to find love as a queer person because of the statistical odds and that, yes, I didn't get any training from real life or media on dating as a queer woman. But this ended up blinding me to something more fundamental: that a lot of my insecurities stemmed from sexual shame, not necessarily because I was queer.

I may have discovered myself straightaway in identity politics (and I am truly glad I skipped the oh-shit-I'm-an-abomination-this-isn't-normal phase), but my identity as a queer person soon became a bit of a shield to protect myself from the turbulence that comes with one's private life, in the world of love, in the world of sex. I didn't take my steps into these worlds because it got easy to foreground my queerness and ignore the fact that I wanted love and sex as a person, not for the sake of ideology. And somewhere, it was easy to ignore it because I have, in many ways, been taught to think of relationships and sex as an indulgent and unimportant. It was easier to say I was queer and think it was socially and politically relevant, than to say I was queer and I wanted to know more people like me to befriend or date. Even when I tried to create a safe space in college, my first fear was, 'What if people think I'm doing this just to find people to date?' To be seen as wanting love and pleasure at the most basic human level—that's an emotional shame no one seemed to be talking about. Even the most woke of people around me would never be caught dead admitting to actively looking for intimacy (ahem, ahem, Tinder shamers). To admit to being lonely was to let down 'the cause'.

I think my turning point for acknowledging and dealing with this shame first-hand happened when I joined Tinder.

I owe Tinder Bhai a lot. It was my first and best wingman and pushed me to do what I desired in my private life more than anyone else. I did catch some flak because of it since not many around me really took Tinder seriously. I first got on it during an exchange programme abroad because it was so far away from home. I even managed to bring my date over for dinner at my dorm, and overcame that fear of being seen as a sexual dating being. Back in India, it took some time and (yet another) glorious heartbreak to push me back into the dating world. Tinder allowed me to see myself as a queer being, but through a more personal lens. I sexted for the first time. Went on dates. Learnt to gauge and express interest. Sent pictures of the moon. Talked. Talked a lot. I not only started learning how people find sexual or romantic partners but also ended up meeting a lot of queer women I had these personal conversations with—conversations I never realised I needed to have. Tinder made me overcome my shame of actively wanting more queer friends and made me take the first trembling steps to a support group. I don't know how to express the utter relief that came with being able to do these without berating myself for 'asking for too much'. I wish there was an easy way to explain to the world that wanting intimacy isn't shameful, to tell my mother that my lovers are as important to me as family and that Tinder is my favourite place sometimes. I've never been ashamed of being queer, but the moral obligation we attach to queer persons—expecting them to change the world and explain themselves to everyone else, or to present themselves as trophies for assimilation—compelled me to craft an image for myself that made it easy to ignore my desires and let in shame. When I realised I was queer, I learnt the language of identity politics not just to find myself in it but also because I felt I'd never be accepted into the queer community without it. But somewhere it failed me because it allowed me to hide my innermost desires for love and intimacy behind it. While I owe identity politics a lot, and I understand the need to define yourself within it, I still hope every queer person finds the peace that comes with acknowledging yourself as a person with love and desire like everyone else. In a world bent on politicising and othering us, even if only with the goal of 'acceptance', it helps to give yourself that space.

It's still hard, but I'm learning to do things like hold my girlfriend's hand at Marine Drive without feeling weird, getting comfortable at being cheesy and not judging people for being the same. I'm learning to prioritise love. I have always been told that family and work is priority and love is second-hand *maal*. That I'm a lesser person for wanting it. But I am unlearning. I am far more comfortable with hickeys showing and living peacefully in my private life without theorising too much about it or turning it into another queer art project. I guess I am now getting better at being a quieter queer.

Earlier, I used to see queer people who were just living their lives without making too much of a hoo-haa about their identity and felt annoyed by them. I thought they weren't doing their duty by not being political about it. But lately, when I see such people, I feel a reassurance and a certain liberation. To be reminded that whatever my identity is, I am, at the end of the day, a person like everyone else.

Debasmita is a queer Mumbai-based researcher, designer and illustrator who has worked in the sexual and reproductive health and rights (SRHR) field for over five years. Currently pursuing an MA in women's studies from TISS, she is interested in queer history, feminist research and communication for social change through storytelling, digital media and art. She wrote this essay while working at Agents of Ishq.

Main Apni Sabse Favourite Hoon: Chronicles of an Instaspam Queen

What is it about being a woman on Instagram that is so joyous, so satisfying—and so annoying to men?

SNEHA ANNAVARAPU

25 April 2019

Here was yet another straight man telling me that I Instagram 'too much'. The fifth man in the past two years. I squinted and continued eating my stone-cold sushi in stone-cold silence, trying not to let my annoyance show, for this was someone I was beginning to catch those dreaded feelings of attachment and fondness for. And, yet, he here he was, almost choking on his wine to convince me that he was right in being 'sceptical' of my Instagramming. It was bad enough that I posted at least a photo a day, I also put up stories—what sort of a vain monster was I? He claimed he wasn't going to stop me from being who I am (oh, the benevolence) but he was 'curious' about why I needed to share so much of my everyday life with my 500+ followers. 'Why do you need so many people telling you you're awesome … don't you know that already?' I was confused. Was this a compliment, a jibe or a passive-aggressive attack stemming from an insecurity about my awesomeness? Before I could begin to snipe back at the question, he smiled. A dazzling, charming smile that made me feel guilty about my Instagram habits. Yet again.

Strangely enough, that didn't stop me from Instagramming as manically as I have been for about two years now. Sure, in that moment, I felt hurt, but what can I do? I don't otherwise feel anything specific about myself when I post on Instagram. I do it out of a very manageable need to communicate—a need that I do *not* want to clamp down on. How do I explain to this sceptical man, I often wondered, that I just like instantly sharing my thoughts, feelings, photographs, jokes and angst with my small world of friends? Over time, my Instagram habits became the butt of all his jibes at me—in front of his friends, in fights over academic disagreements, in jest, in all seriousness. He called me obsessive—a charge I surrendered to, if only to end the conversation, all the while wondering why he was so obsessed with my obsession. Predictably, we broke up, and I triumphantly put up a selfie to celebrate that moment of liberation. Considering how selfies irked him more than any other posts of mine, I was hardly left with a choice.

A few months after feeling guilty about ruining a fledgling relationship, in part due to my unstoppable Instagramming, it occurred to me that had I *not* Instagrammed at all, there would be a different complaint: you *don't* post because you're insecure. I Instagrammed this piece of wisdom promptly. After all, who would consider it breaking news that women are constantly surveilled, evaluated, assessed through the eyes of men who feel authorised to express an opinion no one sought in the first place? But this was hardly the first time I had been shamed about my Instagramming. And it certainly won't be the last.

The first man who thought that I posted too much told me that I have a tendency to 'instaspam'. A genuine lover of a good wordplay, I found the term a total riot, and even put it up on my profile. 'Instaspammer,' I called myself. Mr One was taken aback and even admitted, two years later, that he thought I would've felt bad. What I did not tell him was that I did feel deeply hurt, and deleted Instagram for a week, suddenly very self-conscious of how I was coming across. Maybe I was speaking too much, a trait of mine that is often mocked by friends and family alike, albeit half-seriously: 'Oh, how much she talks! Nobody can shut her up!' Mr One had reminded me that I should feel guilty about saying too much, speaking too much, having too much of a presence. For a few days after getting Instagram back in my life, I was very self-conscious. Just as self-conscious as when I first wore a spaghetti top at the age of twelve and my friend's mother asked me why I wanted to show so much of my body. Thankfully, unlike before, I was able to shrug it off and get back in the Instagram game with as much abandon as before. Women that I narrated this story to reminded me that I am a sociologist. Isn't this annoyance at women 'saying too much', women having 'too much' fun, being 'too pleased with themselves' merely representing the fears of men who want to define the terms of *our* engagement with the world?

I conveyed as much to Mr Two, a fellow academic, who said he thought that was 'too easy' an answer. Mr Two is a deep thinker, a philosopher, a theorist. As if the academic smirk that emerged as I was trying to explain that I Instagram 'for fun' was not enough of a response, he insisted on articulating his thoughts: what about teenagers who are growing up in the age of narcissism? All these selfies, these poses, this obsession with making one's skin appear brighter … all this points to an obsession with oneself and, by ignoring that, I was being unfair to all those genuinely concerned about an obsession with vanity. (There it was again, the equivalent of, 'There are children starving in Bangladesh'—the apocalypse that women will bring upon the world if they did something for fun.) I asked him if he had ever talked to teenagers who were posting these selfies about why they did so. He seemed unsure about why that mattered. Their intentions don't change the detrimental effects of narcissism, he explained patiently to an Instaspammer, while I watched him fall deeper in love with how smart he was.

I didn't give up. I asked him if he thinks that we should not let people express themselves in whatever fashion they want. He grunted. 'We all know everyone overcompensates on this app because they want validation ... everyone who posts too much is basically just deeply vain, insecure—probably both!' He seemed pleased with his own analysis. I indulged him. What I did not tell him then, and I wish I had, was that countless women I knew considered him vain and insecure. Perhaps if we could get him to stop loving his own velvety voice at academic conferences, he would shut up and let others speak. Who said vanity or insecurity was only about one's appearance?

Enter Mr Three. Heart at first sight. A self-hating academic (I had decided to stay away from the intellectual bros) and a lover of visual art. An Instagrammer. Whew, I thought to myself. Mr Three Instagrammed what he considered scenes worth capturing. Sunsets. Skylines. An obscure street. A sculpture. Strangers. Candles. Sunsets. Sunsets. Sunsets. No captions, no people—captions are tacky and nobody was as interesting as he. My face certainly was not worth capturing. My posts were not worth liking (one had to *earn* his Instagram affection). My photography skills were not sophisticated enough to capture his fantastic self. He was the authority, after all, on what is a good click. I couldn't just *demand* validation because we were together. How could I be so precocious? All this thought about who should like what on Instagram, by the way, from someone who claimed to 'not care' about any of this. For eight months, I felt real pressure to aspire to a standard that would befit His Highness. I bent over backwards to take pictures with 'the right frame', I willed myself to hate filters, I took care to strive for symmetry, I ditched photo captions and I shunned selfies (the horror!). No matter what I did though, I was told, 'Surely, you can do better.' Ironically enough, the moment we ended our toxic intimacy, I instantly took better pictures. I was no longer afraid of being judged. Sometimes, his crisp voice haunts me: *Women are being fooled by these tech companies ... the revolution will not occur if women keep taking selfies ... why does this woman post so many photos of herself ... and why do you encourage that by liking her every post ... if you like everyone's pictures, your 'like' doesn't mean anything ... why do you post so often ... why, why, why ...*

And whenever this voice pervades my insides with its seductive tenor, I tell myself: If you don't account for everything you do and prove it is worthwhile by some standards, then whatever you do is deemed worthless.

With these experiences in mind, Mr Four was a lovely surprise. He said he *loved* my Instagram account. It's so full of life, he said. In four weeks, however, he was condescendingly amused. So amused that it bordered on disbelief. Surely I was slacking off at work; surely I was doing *nothing* else but Instagramming; surely, I was not reading enough; surely I was not writing enough; surely ... I had no hobbies. Words, I realised, would hardly allay amusement. I added one task to my ever-expanding daily activity list: get rid of this naysayer. If nothing, he would be impressed with my ability to do multiple things at once: to be able to dump him while posting a click of myself looking relieved.

I was officially tired of being viewed with suspicion: how are you a PhD student if you're not slaving away at your research, feeling the pathos of the entire world, shouldering the responsibility of being a 'critical thinker'? Why, dear aspiring sociologist with an entire dissertation to write, are you Instaspamming?

If anyone cared enough to ask me, I would tell them that I think it's great fun to share moments of my life that I think are worth sharing with a set of people. Do I think that there's a lot in my life that's worth sharing? Yes, probably. Why? I've always been like this—eager to tell you about my life. My writing too has always been derivative of my personal experiences, and I've never quite shied away from thinking through my own experiences and finding moments that might resonate with others. Beyond this, I haven't felt the need to excavate my own behaviour. Why can't I have my own compulsions, my own compulsiveness? Why do I have to lay bare my 'behaviour' and make sense of my actions as if I was obliged to the Ghosts of Boyfriends Past?

That a very satisfying answer to my existential woes was waiting around the corner was a good surprise to me. About a month ago, a male friend commented that his Instagram stories are too obviously gendered: most of them are by women. It irked him that here too men watched women. Women perform, like belly dancers, and men gaze at them; women feel the pressure of being watched, and go about pleasing the male gaze, he lamented. Of course, I too have noticed the skewed nature of Instagram posting, especially with selfies (which is why it gives me unbridled joy when I see a man post a selfie).

But his observation made me realise that I like Instagram for exactly the reason he was feeling 'troubled' by: I love the fact that most of my content and newsfeed is *by* women. I like the fact that women take up space on Instagram. I like that women share their outfits, their thoughts, their feelings, their faces, their coffee, their dogs, their cats, their shoes, their hair, their heartbreak, their mimosas, their sunrises, their sunsets, their nights and their gaze. I like that women post about their heartbreak, that women post screenshots of men being shitty to them, that women can follow other women who inspire them or just make them laugh. I like that I can *like* all this. That it's a world defined by what pleases these women—their amusements, their pastimes, their insecurities, their desire to be admired or their wish for community.

And it breaks my heart when I see number of women on my newsfeed *apologise* when they post 'too much', *apologise* for selfies, *apologise* for wanting to share moments of their life, *apologise* for having a presence. Every time I see a woman add a little apologetic disclaimer about how she is seeking validation 'because she is having a bad day', that little Instagram heart seems a bit broken. Perhaps mending that broken heart requires us to own up to our desires. Most women are told that 'wanting to be looked at' is wrong. We have been told from our childhood that we must hunch our backs, cower our heads, walk quickly and not garner attention. It's not safe, it's not right, it's not something 'good women' do.

In the virtual streets, we are still figuring out our presence, our participation, on our own terms. But once we are walking these virtual streets, let's not be shy or skulk away from being what we want to be, from being seen the way we want to be seen, from loitering, or shouting from the rooftops.

When not teaching young adults in Singapore the pleasures and possibilities of a sociological imagination, Sneha can be spotted taking selfies in many an autorickshaw in Hyderabad while having the most profound conversations with the drivers. For a more coherent version of this self-description, please visit www.snehanna.com.

My Struggle To Live and Love With Vaginismus

I used to fail at maths. And now it seemed I was failing at sex. But was I?

TARA

4 October 2020

I have primary vaginismus. I have said this out loud to hardly anyone because of the shame and stigma that is associated with experiencing what comes with vaginismus—the inability to allow vaginal penetration. There are many contributing factors to vaginismus, but in my case, it is a manifestation of trauma in my body. My brain perceives physical contact, particularly the act of penetration or insertion of any object in my body, as a potential threat, and freezes. My heart desires pleasure, intimacy, love and sex. Yet I am constantly in a state of hypervigilance, scanning for signs of danger. Forming a connection with an intimate partner or relaxing during a gynaecological exam feels impossible. This is not merely all in my head. I cannot relax because my body and mind do not know how to feel safe.

I was in a long-term relationship with a man I met in college for many years. We enjoyed a rich intimate life. He read stories and poetry out loud to me. We were both exploring the sexual world for the first time, with each other. Every night, I would go up to his hostel room where we made out passionately, explored each other's bodies and cuddled. We had oral sex and shared many intimate moments. When our relationship became long-distance, we had phone sex. Much later, I learnt that none of this was 'real' for him—he would tell his friends that we were together, but we had never had sex. When he shared this with me, I felt ashamed, angry and betrayed. For me, he is and will always be the man I had sex with for the first time. I experienced orgasms and, together, we discovered sexual acts that we both enjoyed. Just because he did not penetrate my body does that mean we did not have sex? I was mortified by how other people who are having penetrative sex would perceive me. He had decided everything for us—our future, the validity of our sexual experience and our break-up.

It was his decision to not have penetrative sex. There were no condoms in his bedroom, and when I had offered to buy some, he said he preferred not to have penetrative sex. One day, he also said that we could never be together because we belonged to different faiths. He said that he did not want to be the one I have sex with for the first time. Was sex only penetration? Was I only my vagina? It was troubling and hurtful that someone I loved so deeply didn't seem to take my desires and choices into consideration. But somehow, caught up in that relationship, I too started believing that I never had real sex. So, I never realised I have vaginismus.

I remember though, that even when he tried to insert his finger into my vagina, it would wall up, like it had a mind of its own. I felt disconnected from my own body part, but I never gave it much thought. I wonder often now, what would have happened if we had had penetrative sex and I couldn't proceed. Would he have been frustrated? Upset?

Agitated? Or thought that I was just making a fuss about something routine?

Growing up, my mother had told me about periods, and a special teacher visited our school to tell only the girls how babies are made without explaining what sex is, how it happens and what different people experience while having sex. When regular people spoke about sex, it seemed a given that penetration, for women, is a painful experience, that there would be blood—something my partner also brought up. I would curiously ask my college friends about their first penetrative experience—most had been sexual for the first time, all with men. Some would never talk about it. Most would be taciturn. I wasn't looking for juicy details or prying. I was simply trying to understand what intercourse would entail. The fear was palpable, though I had no idea that I had vaginismus. When there is so much silence about sex, when it's already presented as a difficult experience for women, the chances of discovering that there may be an issue that isn't just in your mind are slim.

I also grew up in a violent home environment, feeling constantly unsafe. As a child with a learning disability, my body bore scars of beatings, and my mind remained in a state of constant hypervigilance, anticipating violent outbursts. One can live through suffering and pain, and understand what it means. But not having the language for your pain can leave you feeling very lost. That is how I felt growing up—lost and alone.

I learnt I had vaginismus in a very vulnerable state. I had broken up with my partner. His family did not approve of our match, and he gave up on convincing them because *khoon ka rishta hai*. After nine years of trying and trying to make this relationship work, we ended it.

I was in a difficult financial condition; I was supporting myself, my family and cradling my broken heart. There was no time to grieve and mourn this loss. I moved overseas and started a new job, learning to live by myself, trying to move on and meet new people. For the first time, I downloaded dating apps. I was thirty.

When I thought I was ready, I connected with someone on Facebook, and we became friendly. But when he showed interest in becoming intimate, I completely shut him off. I told myself that perhaps I was not over my break-up. The fear of pain had taken deep root in my heart. But we met again after a gap, and somehow, this young man and I kissed. After a few minutes, he asked me if I was ready and I nodded, my heart beating frantically against my chest. *Was* I ready? He put on a condom but the moment he tried to penetrate me, I felt a sharp and searing pain at the opening of my vagina. It was like my vagina screamed at his penis without consulting me.

I immediately asked him to stop. I wanted to burst into tears, I was so embarrassed. He was confused, but still ready, and asked me eagerly, 'Are you really sure we cannot do this?'

I shook my head. 'Sorry, we just can't.'

I wondered why though. Was it because he was only the second person I was being intimate with? Or because I needed more than a casual connection? But really, the fears that had haunted me during my first sexual experience had followed me to a new place, to a new person. I was afraid of being hurt, bruised, of my sense of safety being violated.

He was a kind friend and hung out with me for a few days. We kissed and made out during my stay, but he kept saying that he needed to have penetrative sex to 'finish'. I began to feel like I was causing, and perhaps would continue to cause, men to not 'finish.' I had learnt from the media and friends that this was 'climax', the culmination of a linear story of sex. Things get hot and heavy, people make passionate love; there are no hiccups, no one gets embarrassed, no one cries, no one fails to have sex.

But me? I used to fail at maths, and now, I was failing at sex. I was dejected and heartbroken. I tried to speak to a friend at work, but all she said was, 'Oh, maybe you have not found the right person yet.'

How was I going to find that person? The world of online dating felt so intimidating. When people—cis-het men, anyway—are looking for sex on the Internet, they don't expect to meet a person whom they cannot enter. I feared that if I tried dating, I would get a person excited, and then right before penetration, I would say, 'I'm in the mood, but my vagina is not.' Is there a guide book for having this conversation?

I Googled, *fear of penetrative sex ... not able to have sex*.

There it came. A label. *Vaginismus*.

Some time passed before I looked for a non-invasive and queer-affirmative gynaecologist in Mumbai. It was my first time going to a gynaecologist. I had only heard horror stories of women being asked personal questions. Having vaginismus was terrifying enough without also fielding intrusive questions from doctors.

But I went, determined to be confident, to not be bullied. I told her I had been with two men but found penetrative sexual intercourse too painful, that I'd never inserted a tampon or even met a gynaecologist before. She wrote down 'primary vaginismus' and asked the nurse to bring out the dilators. Three dilators, ranging from the size of my little finger to big, penis-shaped ones, were placed in front of me. The sight terrified me. She reassured me that we would try, but didn't have to continue if it was hard: 'I just need to see if you can.' The moment the dilator inched closer to me, I raised my buttocks, my muscles clenched and my vaginal walls closed. The doctor asked me to breath and relax: 'Imagine you are urinating.' Somehow, that did the trick. For the very first time, something went into my vagina. 'See!' she exclaimed. At first numb with fear, I was now numb with joy. My vaginal walls relaxed. Dilator number two was inserted. The third one went halfway through, and I asked her to stop as we had agreed. Having something in my vagina was strange—there was no bleeding and the two smaller dilators slid in and out with the help of a water-based gel lubricant.

For the first time in my life, my vagina was listening to me. We were on the same page; it had decided to open up to me. It felt like it belonged to me, and did not exist outside of my bodily and emotional experience. I tried using my dilators every day. The first time was hard. Whatever I tried, my muscles would involuntarily clench. I would breathe, apply a lot of lubricant and gently persist.

At the same time, I also started receiving therapy. As a trauma survivor of my violent childhood, my challenges are further compounded. But I was learning to anchor myself to the present, learning to be safe. I started reading a lot about vaginismus, trauma, and people suffering from trauma who also experience vaginismus. I had terms for what was going on in my mind and in my body. This made me feel less alone.

My sister was the first person I shared this with. She was very kind, sharing that her first time with penetrative sex had been uncomfortable and painful: 'I only had sex because I was at the age where I felt I needed to tell my close friends I had done "it".'

My therapist was the other person I told, explaining my response to touch. When I told her I was scared of being in relationships and telling men that I have vaginismus, she validated my fears. We discussed how I could go out there, look for love, look for sex, with vaginismus. My therapist also asked me to try masturbating and explore what seems fun and pleasurable.

I tell many of my friends that I am struggling to be intimate with men, and they listen, but I don't know if they understand. I still cannot tell anyone that I have vaginismus. It becomes a label—they read the label and based on their understanding of sex, they draw a conclusion about my sexual life.

Am I in a relationship with someone? A man? No. But I am learning to have a relationship with myself, with my body. I feel more in control because I am now on dilator number three of Amielle Comfort. I have had to unlearn many ideas I had about sex in order to rebuild my relationship with pleasure. I had to tell myself that I am having sexual experiences. I wanted to see the different ways in which I can learn pleasure. So, I bought a clitoris-stimulating vibrator and used that to have orgasms. Watching porn was frustrating. Everyone 'climaxes' in porn. The fixed journey, the predictable, linear sexual path starts to heighten my anxiety about lacking something essential. But I searched for other eroticism and started listening to audio stories on Dipsea. Of course, there is a sense of linearity for the characters in these stories too, but at least I am able to create a personal sexual experience in my mind while masturbating.

When I had just begun dilating, I joined an online support group—a community of people which also includes partners of those who have had vaginismus. Many women and individuals share their stories, their dilating journeys, their frustration and lack of motivation to dilate. Sometimes, we also celebrated each other's journeys. We understand so keenly how a person feels when they have been able to manage penetrative sex and enjoy it. In that community, I do not feel alone. But the world outside can be very isolating, intimidating and limiting.

Now that I feel more comfortable with myself, I recently told another friend, and the more people I share this with, the more my shame shatters into pieces. Its silence is broken. This friend was wonderful; I took pictures of my dilators and shared them with her to tell her which dilator I am on. She said, 'I completely understand. Penetrative sex is difficult, and sometimes you do feel frozen.' She does not have vaginismus, but listening to her made me realise that maybe sex is not always as easy as porn and films make it sound, is it?

So, I am carving on my own path. I started a personal blog in which I write about my sexual experiences with myself, my fantasies filled with delicious possibilities and my mental health. Recently, I wrote a private blog post describing my imaginary sexual experience with my dentist on whom I have a massive crush. We're in a fantastical land, and this dentist is loving, caring and makes me feel safe. In this fantasy we do not have penetrative sex—but it is hot, pleasurable, fun and we are happy at the end of it. We know that there will be more, but in my fantasy, in this specific story, we are happy with how it is now. I am still trying to muster the courage to ask him out, but I am not feeling hindered because of vaginismus. I'm just scared that he will find it absurd that I am asking him on a date after he's pulled out my teeth!

I don't control my vagina, or feel ashamed or embarrassed by it. It is scared. It needs me—to love it and to comfort it, and to slowly help it feel safe. It needs to know it is cared for.

The Prostitute and the Saviour

I was a product in a meat market

ARINA ALAM
November 2020

It was February 2020 when I left prostitution. I had come to sex work in a very confused manner—confused in the sense that I didn't know that sex work was the last option I had to survive in Chandigarh.

I was evicted from my lodgings. I had been homeless for a few hours and made a hundred calls to people I knew very well and very little, but didn't get a response. I got to know about Khajeri (in Chandigarh) from a friend and the work one had to do there. I remember taking an autorickshaw to Khajeri and talking over the phone to a man I didn't know well; he kept warning me against going there. He said that he would find me a place to live and help me find a job. 'No gentlemen or women go to Khajeri,' he said. I didn't want to go there. I didn't want to go anywhere. I just wanted to get off the autorickshaw and enjoy a day to myself in a luxury hotel, doing nothing. I had five thousand rupees in savings. But I finally went to Khajeri because I knew very well that the five thousand wouldn't last long.

When I first saw Khajeri, I compared it to Sonagachi in Kolkata. I don't know where this vivid mental image came from. I have neither visited Sonagachi nor watched anything related to it. I had only read about how Sonagachi is Asia's number one red-light district and had heard a few things from my male cousins who visited there. But Khajeri felt like a mini-Sonagachi. It has a rustic quality that Chandigarh's posh localities do not. It reminded me of the small mofussil where I spent my childhood. If you remove all the hotels from Khajeri, it will look just like a mofussil of the 1990s where you can hear music coming from the radio and shops selling fake fairness cream and other cheap 'duplicate' products. Khajeri can't afford originality yet, even in 2020.

I liked the initial days: the Bihari neighbourhood, the smell of gutkha, the muddy roads. The coming and going of men—their smell, their touch, their symmetrical and asymmetrical faces and bodies, their different socio-economic statuses and the stories of loneliness they wrote on my bare skin. Above all, the money was easy in prostitution. I never thought my body could be used as a medium of income and someone could make a profit out of it. My gender dysphoria had only ever taught me to hate my body. But sex work instilled a sense of pride in my body. I started feeling beautiful because of the attention I was getting from men.

The initial feelings of pleasure were quickly lost though. I felt suffocated by the environment. I felt I needed to get away from prostitution. Many men were nice—but not all the men who paid were kind. They were paying for something, so they wanted 'full pleasure' even if it meant torturing me. And I began to feel guilty about sleeping with so many men. I'd been in a happy, monogamous relationship before I came to Khajeri, and kept thinking of my ex's handsome face.

I was a product in a meat market, my brown skin was coated in stick foundation. My body was roasted by men's lusts and was served for them to savour. Every day, I watched the stars with vacant eyes before standing on the road like a leg of lamb. The touch of men started tearing at me. I felt like a thousand hands were trying to tear me apart and make a feast of my raw meat. Sleeping under them, I couldn't bear the heaviness anymore. All the faces were a blur, all the bodies turned into a bulb of meat. Even the sculpted male body was not arousing anymore.

I left Khajeri in February 2020 with the help of a man. I met him online. There was every reason for me to believe in him. The most important reason was that he was not ashamed to be seen with me in public. I realise that people are embarrassed to walk with me. Even my trans friends, whether open or closeted, try to avoid me in public for fear of their identity being disclosed. But this man did not just dare to take me outside, he was introducing me to his friends and requesting them to offer me a job or helping me plan how to make my crowdfunding appeal successful for my gender-affirming surgery. He took me to every job interview I had and stood outside interview halls until I finished. He was trying to find a safe locality for me. He was not like the other men in my life who only took from me. I liked this friendship with an older man. It was unique and cute. I can't think of an appropriate word to describe my feelings.

So, when he first forcibly kissed me, I just tolerated it as an act of gratitude even though I was repulsed. I was looking for a friend in him or a supportive fatherly figure. But he was looking at me as the glue that could put the pieces of his heart together, the person he would save to redeem himself. He used to spend long nights telling me how lonely he was or how he is in a failed marriage. Soon, he realised that I had begun to feel irritated by his presence, his touch, his sad stories. But instead of understanding my consent and how I responded to the age gap between us, he began to say things such as how, with my looks, I shouldn't expect a handsome young man. He told me that I was not sensitive enough to be called a woman. He said that the doctor who delayed my surgery did the right thing, as I didn't have feminine qualities yet.

I walked out of the one-sided relationship with all my strength and lost half the money I had. To be honest, I miss the man, yet I am afraid of his touch.

I am now trying to get a job and be a part of society. But I am afraid the situation is really hard for everyone. With the little savings I had and with the help of friends, I am still living a good life. I don't know how long this will last and when I may go back to prostitution, no matter how hard I try not to. But for now, this is me.

Arina Alam is a twenty-seven-year-old transwoman. She says she is a person with lots of mental limitations and fights her mind every day. On some days, she wins, and on others, she loses. The only happiness she gets is from writing.

I Came Out to My Mom and Now I Think She's Fomosexual

A mother's totally unexpected response to her daughter's coming out.

SHARVARI SASTRY

22 August 2017

'Achha, Ma, I have something to tell you ...'

We were sprawled diagonally on the L-shaped sofa, and in all appearances, it seemed like just another day in the life of a diasporic desi daughter. It had been four days since my annual trip home. The novelty had worn off, and nightly chats dwindled. My mother had resumed her favourite post-dinner activity: Facebook Feed Analysis + Commentary.

'*Haan toh bolo na,* I'm listening,' she said, still peering into her phone. *Puddup puddup.* My mother was liking things vigorously. Maybe that was a good sign.

'It might seem very shocking.' I had rehearsed and revised this preamble a million times on my long flight back.

'Nothing shocks me.' Still not looking up, still liking.

'Okay. Achha, so. I'm seeing someone ... means, dating someone ... means, relationship.' The practised script was fast fleeing from my brain, causing a loud pounding in my chest as it galloped away.

As she finally looked up, her expression was a mixture of mild concern and extreme, genuine relief. 'Arre, that's great! I'm so happy for you! Very good. What's shocking about that?'

What indeed? My mother had dispassionately observed my prolonged, uneventful long-distance relationship with a boy from college, offering neither advice nor criticism. That was three years ago. As far as she was concerned, there had been no men of romantic significance in my life since then. And she was right.

She prodded on impatiently, phone forgotten. 'So? Who is it?'

'So, that's the thing. The person I'm seeing … it is not a gents. It is a ladies.'

I was trying to find the most non-sexual term to describe a woman. In retrospect, a noun commonly used to refer to bathroom spaces was probably a stupid choice. Anyway.

'Oh.'

I had expected her to be angry, but she just looked confused. This I could handle. Mostly everyone I had told had responded with some stage of polite puzzlement.

'Oh? So have you always been, *ya ki States jaake hua?*'

'Oh? So what about that guy you were with?'

'Oh? So how do you people actually, you know, like, do stuff?'

'Oh? So you just realised? I always suspected this about you.'

My mother was clearly experiencing all these questions at the same time. I magnanimously offered to guide her out of perplexity. 'Ma, don't worry. I haven't told many people. It is a lot to handle, I understand. Take your time. We can talk about it. Tell me what you are thinking.'

Long pause. I steeled myself for a lecture about society, morals, family, nature, motherhood, tick-tock biological clock, etc.

'Hmm,' she began. 'Hmm. Achha, tell me one thing, how do you know the difference?'

'The difference?'

'You know. The difference. Between friendship and something more. How do you know that you are *ahem* ... attracted?'

'I don't know, Ma. It is just a feeling.'

'Feeling? *Waise toh,* I've also had feelings,' advanced my mother. 'You know, sometimes I also feel—ladies, they are just better ...'

I had mentally prepared myself for every type of feeling I thought my mother could possibly have—angry-feeling, sad-feeling, betrayed-feeling, scared-feeling, *log-kya-kahenge*-feeling—but this homophilic fellow-feeling was totally off-script.

'Haan, ladies are very nice. You know, they understand each other. They have the same problems—periods, patriarchy ...' I tried to make vague general comments to veer the conversation away from any more talk of feelings. But my mother's concentration was now wholly focused on Lesbian Life Analysis + Commentary.

'Your *friend* ... she's also ...?'

'Gay? Yes, she is.'

'Hmm. In my hostel also there were some girls who were ... you know ... very close. No one said anything, but we all knew. Always doing ghuss-phuss together, always giggling.'

She paused. On her face, I saw a profound realisation dawning.

'So does this mean that you ...' she said slowly '... does this mean you *never* have to deal with men?'

'Not *never* ...'

'But never in ... personal-type situations?'

'I guess not.'

'You are lucky. Men are useless.'

My mother's face was contorting into a kaleidoscope of expressions that was strangely familiar. I had encountered that face somewhere else before. It was the look that many of my undergraduate students wore on Friday evenings when, instead of underage over-the-top partying, they were forced to sit for yet another research methodologies tutorial. Unmistakably, it was that singular combination of premature retrospection, pre-emptive nostalgia and utter despair. But what was it doing here on my mother's face? Could it be ...? Did my mother have ... FOMO?

'And you will never have to get married also?'

'It probably won't be possible, legally ... 377 ...'

'Wow, you are very lucky. Marriage is also useless.'

I knew what was coming. A diatribe on the Many Forms of Marital Distress was my mother's conception of girl talk. It began with the usual, 'Look at me. Highly educated, highly qualified, with two full-time jobs. One at work and one at home. Cooking, cleaning, making the bed, washing the clothes, who will do all this? I only have to do it na ...'

But today, instead of ending on a note of resignation, she began to bubble over into righteous dismay.

'Why should I do it? I never chose this life! In my time, we didn't have any choices. Happy *ki* unhappy, who cares? What other options are there?'

I was not sure if this was a rhetorical question.

'But there can be na!' she roared on. Clearly it was.

'See in that film *Fire*—those women's husbands? Totally useless! But at least they are nice to each other. I still remember that one scene, where one lady is massaging the other's feet with so much love. You think that can happen ever with men? No way! You've seen your father, can't even carry his own plate back into the kitchen, forget anything else.'

I made a noise that was intended to be a sympathetic cluck, but it came out sounding like an impatient groan.

'No point in complaining,' she continued. 'I can't change anything now. But you go'

'Go where?'

'Means go and do your thing.'

'Okay, thanks for the support, but I'm not going anywhere.'

I put her foot on my knee and started to press above the heel, the way I knew she liked. My mother slid back into the cushions and picked up her phone again. *Puddup puddup puddup.*

Sharvari Sastry is an educator and idli enthusiast who likes to spend her time reading, singing and doing jigsaw puzzles.

Travel With Me

KIRAN KAKADE

I'd travel kilometres on your chest with my lips,
Maybe hop onto a train once,
and at other times,
board the many trams along the road of your neck …
ticketless.
'Catch me.'
Each time I escape being caught, I'll open a button of your shirt.

I'd sit pillion while you ride us on the highway,
Become the driver when we're passing by the beaches.
The waves will come from the sea,
But they'll hit your shore.

When we're driving through the desert, and your wheels are in my hands,
I don't think
we'll need water.
I'll kiss your lips and you'll see a mirage.

The stormy skies may perhaps feel insecure, watching us
fiercely rub our bodies against each other.
The dark clouds of our souls will clash, and
I'll gasp.
Each breath sounding like thunder, its decibels
increasing with the speed and intensity

Of each strike of your lightning.
'Don't stop.'
And yet,
it will rain somewhere else.

Kiran Kakade is a poet and artist who swims in intimacies, grief and tenderness while exploring politics and unweaving the norms of being and loving. They also work on mental health, social justice and disability rights.

SEX ACTUALLY

Encounters Women Can't Forget

Women make sense of their diverse sexual experiences

It was 2018. Barely a year ago, #MeToo had blown the lid off women's sexual experiences and revealed how much sexual violation existed in workplaces, in colleges and among friends. For the first time, women's granular sexual experiences filled the public domain. Then came the Aziz Ansari case, where an online journal published a piece by a young woman on her sexual encounter with Ansari. It unleashed a debate on whether what had happened was bad sex or non-consensual sex. If anything, the story revealed how much non-consensuality and detachment were actually an accepted part of everyday heterosexual sex.

For us, it opened up a question: how could we move past describing violence, towards changing it? How could a new conversation about freedom, equality and respect arise from these revelations?

To us it seemed that at least one part of what this required was to be able to talk about sex not as a homogenous concept, but as a heterogenous experience. When it comes to sexual experiences, especially of women and queer people, there is a speed with which the law, social communities and the media decide on their validity and meaning, marshalling them to serve their own pre-existing definitions of right and wrong, crime and punishment.

The voices of women describing their sexual experiences on their terms painted a complex understanding of women's sexual realities. And these also suggested new understandings and ideas of consent, healing, justice, violence, autonomy and relationships, intertwining the personal and political in a constant, mutually changing dynamic. To make space for this new conversation, it seemed important to talk about sex not only as a concept, but sex as it actually happens.

So, we partnered with the pioneering feminist website The Ladies Finger to begin this conversation. We invited women to contribute a story about a sexual experience they couldn't forget—awful, awesome or ho-hum—anonymously. Nearly a hundred accounts tumbled in—textured, self-aware, funny, wise, angry, sweet, raunchy. In their layers, sexual experience revealed itself as a place of learning, politics, pleasure as well as violence, so much casual violence. The difference was that these writers made sense of their own experiences. Their insights could not easily be slotted in the way the world demands they should. In their polyphony, they pushed against those boundaries of crime and punishment and put together, argued for a more ethical emotional world, a more feminist social world.

The contributors mentioned how old they were at the time of the experience, and how old they were at the time of writing. Those numbers too told their own story. They traced an autonomous journey the writers had made through that sexual experience, offering a form of political reflection.

The accounts in this section are a small selection that represent the wealth of sexual experiences and insights. They record a slice of time that birthed new conversations about sexual autonomy, sexual authenticity and sexual politics.

1. My First Time Taught Me How Not to Have Sex

JASMIN

I was twenty years old and I hadn't had my first kiss.

This was a source of great embarrassment for me. And I worried that as time went by, and I grew older, it would only become stranger and stranger. Most of my close friends were already having sex on a regular basis, and here I was with no experience except for a few drunk kisses shared with female friends.

But then came a wave of Tinder in friends' groups.

All of them were on it, and so was I. It was a bit terrifying for me to venture out there with no experience. Here were people who were 'down to fuck' while I honestly preferred 'let's talk a little and take it as slow as high school kids'.

But I finally met R.

We met somewhere in Bangalore. As we sat beside each other under a tree, I could sense the conversation was just a farce, that he was leading up to kissing me. I didn't even feel connected to him yet. But that was okay. By that point, I just wanted to 'get done' with my first kiss.

He then led me out of the restaurant and as we walked down the street, he asked me to come to a hotel room several times. Each time, I said no.

Then he spotted a park, and I was also eager to kiss, so we went there. But as we made out, his hands went right for my crotch. I stopped him.

They went up my shirt. I let that happen. But I didn't like it.

He was rough, grabbing my breasts like he wanted to just tear them off of me. It hurt, not in a sexy way. Again, his hands went for my crotch. Again, I stopped him. And again, and again, and again, in spite of even telling him verbally to stop.

For the twenty-two-year-old me now, this would be a red flag: a partner unable to understand smaller moments of consent. Forget about even the politics of it. What disturbs me about all these moments when consent is breached is that I imagine myself in the same position.

If a partner shows any discomfort, even the smallest sign, I pick up on it. I stop. I would find no pleasure in continuing something my partner doesn't enjoy. This should've been a red flag, but I was none the wiser then, and so I met him again.

And I did like him a little.

He was funny. I was done with my first kiss. I had met a few other men on Tinder with whom things didn't go very far, apart from kissing. And I thought I was ready for more.

But I must admit, my attitude behind it was still 'Let's just get done with it, let's see how it all works so I'm prepared when the real thing happens'.

I don't find this entirely foolish. It's all right. Sometimes, you want to wait, and sometimes you just want to go for a test run. But I didn't feel like I was completely comfortable or in control with how the test run would go.

Honestly, even though I was eager to just try out the things that come after you take the clothes off, I wished for something slower, gentler, something revelling in the discovery of touch and another person's body. When we entered the hotel room, he had my shirt and bra off in minutes. It was a passion I did not mirror. He was new to me. This all was new to me. I had told him several times that I wanted to take it slow. He had held my hand and said that was fine by him.

Then a few minutes into making out, he was pulling my pants off. I said no. He looked away and frowned, saying, 'Oh, I must be so ugly, that's why you don't want it anymore.' I feel a degree of embarrassment for not calling him out on his bullshit whining right then and there. But in the moment, I was so nervous and so tense that I used an age-old line which was true enough to me—it's not you, it's me! But he continued his drama. I gave in. My pants came off. My panties came off. He asked me why I wasn't getting wet.

By this time I was so confused and dazed at the pace of events that I didn't know what I was doing. It's obvious now that none of it was sexy for me. And that it should've been obvious to him too. And that his teasing lines about how it was because he is ugly or not good enough were ridiculously emotionally manipulative. I still feel embarrassed for giving in to them so easily. But over time, I have also tried to forgive myself for not knowing what I know now only because of that encounter. When I read the story a girl recently wrote about having her worst date with Aziz Ansari, I cried.

I cried when she described him pushing her hand down to his dick. I cried about how she just gave him a blowjob even though she didn't want to. I cried when she sent the 'I hate men' text to her friend immediately after. Because that's what it felt like with R.

I was into it, to an extent. But it felt as if he was having sex solely for himself. He had no sense of how I was feeling through it all, and couldn't care less. Throughout the night, he kept putting my hand on his dick even when I didn't want to touch him. He would push my head down even when I didn't want to go there. He would use lube because I just wasn't getting wet.

He would eventually penetrate me and ignore me when I said it was hurting too much. After this night, I did not want to be with men for a long time. I was left with this image of sex as something I couldn't like. I was much better off with my own imagination and fingers. I admit I even felt disgusted with myself for a while.

As I understood the ways in which he'd forced me to do things, I also understood that he should have had the sensitivity and ethics to not resort to such methods. And I realised how naïve I was in not recognising them. I'm sure my friends would've called him out the first time he whined, 'Oh, you don't want to go further because I'm ugly.' But I have also forgiven myself.

It took that encounter for me to learn that it's okay to be pedantically clear with how much you want. If you don't want to touch any penises, you don't fucking have to. (If he acts hurt or thinks you're a prude, well, what-fucking-ever.) If you don't want something in your mouth, don't put it in your mouth.

In the age of online dating, there's a certain pressure to be open to 'casual' relationships. My problem is that the definition of 'casual' that most men (that I've met) go by is 'to be almost emotionless'. Showing any sign of affection is terrifying. But I realised this kind of casual isn't for me. It's not that I want someone to be my 'boyfriend', but I want care and affection. And I'm not shy to admit that openly anymore.

Here's a positive side of the story that I'd like to end this on: it would take me two years to meet someone else. In that time, I would have brief stints with people that I never would want to take to bed. But with this person, the physicality feels spiritual. It's leaves me at a loss for words, as if I have no language for it. I want to touch him everywhere, with my hands and my mouth. Sometimes, I want him to take all my clothes off within minutes of the door being closed.

I love touching his penis and giving him blowjobs—for the two years after R, I thought I would always hate that. And I love the way he touches me everywhere. Everything in bed feels like an exploration, a learning and discovery of each other's bodies—where someone is ticklish, where they have moles and birthmarks, the parts of their neck that can send them wild with sucking.

I feel like this is what I had always been looking for (and will continue looking for) in bed. This is what sex means to me now: a co-discovery, revelling in finding out what their touch can do, what your own touch can do.

I don't regret 'getting done with it' when I was with R. I have learnt a lot from that encounter. Most importantly, I've learnt about what I want and what I don't. I've learnt that it isn't really sex that I care for if the other person is treating you like a blow-up doll. More than the moment of orgasm, what turns me on the most is learning about each other, responding to each other, sensing each other.

2. The Chap Who Would Have Made a Good App

CHITRA
Age Then: 25
Age Now: 38

A guy I met on a dating site pursued me for a few weeks, hectically. He was a bit strange because he was five or six years older and had a job but still seemed to have all the time in the world to pursue me on email and SMS and on the site's chat feature. He had a very effective way of sexting that got me very hot and bothered.

Which is why I decided to meet him. As a person, he seemed rather charmless, or maybe I am saying this in retrospect because of what happened with me, and I'd also heard from a few other women he slept with. Or perhaps not—truly, he was rather grey. And I was really meeting him only for sex.

On the day we finally met, he picked me up in his car and drove me to his house. He had lots of books in his living room that overlapped somewhat with stuff I was interested in. I pulled a title off a shelf to look at, and he began to feel me up, sort of like around the book, over the book, under the book. It could have been sexy but I just remember feeling *ki yeh ho kya raha hain, why so urgent, bro?* Then, in five minutes, he'd backed me through his house to his bed. He took my clothes off very rapidly, with great efficiency. I was still slow to respond, and wasn't feeling anything, not even angry. Then, I think he gave me head briskly, kneeling on the floor next to the bed. I suppose I must have stared at the ceiling. And then, swiftly, there came the moment of penetration.

The thing I forgot to mention is that in his dirty talk there were lots of sophisticated implications that he had the perfect penis, that he was an awesome sex machine. Now, here was the moment, but he sort of penetrated and then exited just as rapidly. I looked up to enquire—*sab khairiyat?* But he was looking lost in space. He said, 'I feel haunted by the ghost of my ex-girlfriend.' I felt bad for him for exactly one minute because, before I could even extend any sympathy, he had begun the reverse hustle. Ten minutes later, I was back in my clothes and out of the house and he was driving me back to my place. It was all too clinical and neat for me to throw a big, giant hissy fit, which I should have. Not because he didn't want to have sex but because he was behaving like I was the Aquaguard salesman after he had pursued me for weeks. I don't remember if we continued to speak. We might have because I am sure I felt a lot of pressure to be cool. I see him once in a couple of years because we now have common friends and he finds it hard to make eye contact. I am viciously chatty. I don't think he is like that because he is embarrassed. I think he does believe he is an awesome sex machine but he is just not good with women, or perhaps even human beings in general.

But he was good with sexting. He'd make a good app.

3. Sex is Something Nice Two People Do When They Love Each Other

RITA K.
Age Then: 22
Age Now: 27

My sister used to make this joke about me. 'You're, like, the de-virginator of Mumbai or something.' This was a bit of an exaggeration. What it meant was that by the age of twenty-two, I had had a few decent experiences with sex, all of them with men trying it for the first time. Sometimes it was great, sometimes a bit dull. Nothing excruciating, often sort of fumbling, but mostly earnest and sweet.

Unlike most Indian parents who either don't talk about it at all, or load young women up with the heady cocktail of shame-pregnancy-log-kya-kahenge apocalypse, my dad had explained sex to pre-teen me as 'something nice that two people do when they love each other'. Well, that sounds neat, I'd thought.

So, when I decided to start having sex, it was with a teenage boyfriend I loved very sincerely. We waited for a respectable amount of time into the relationship, talked extensively about our feelings before and after, and read every article we could find on contraception via web browsers in incognito mode. I explained smugly to my still-unsexed friends how we'd avoided first-time pain with seamless expertise. I was well on my way to a happy, fulfilled, sex-positive, feminist lifestyle.

A few years later, I met this guy, let's call him Hari. Hari was my awkward engineer friend. Hari listened while I cried for months after my great teenage love found his own (other) great teenage love. Hari was especially interested in hearing about my exciting experiences with sex. When we met, Hari sometimes stared at my chest, but became abashed and stopped when I told him I had noticed. Hari was sad when he asked me out and I said I didn't see him that way. Hari was angry when I kissed someone else. When I told him that I had slept with this someone else, Hari called me a bitch and stopped talking to me.

But Hari and I eventually became friends again. We dated other people and a few years went by. One day, Hari and I went to a party together. 'Don't hit on me, okay, there are lots of single women here,' I told him. But Hari and I got very drunk and made out. That night, he took me home. On our way there, I said mildly, 'Oh, are we going to have sex then?' Hari said, 'Yup.' After dodging it for years, I found that hooking up with Hari was not as terrible as I had imagined it would be, and I was surprised and relieved.

One of the first few times we were having sex, Hari lay back in bed and said with a smile, 'Now serve me.'

I stopped and looked up, sure he was joking.

'Say that once more, and you'll never see me naked again,' I said coquettishly.

'Don't bring feminism into the bedroom, you'll ruin sex,' he replied, dead serious.

I rolled my eyes and thought, 'Ruin sex for whom, I wonder.' But Hari wasn't a bad guy. Sure, we sometimes disagreed on whether the friendzone was fair or not, but he had come a long way over the years. At least he had stopped saying, 'It isn't rape, just surprise sex, ha ha.'

I was quite sure where the power in this relationship lay. I was young, skinny and conventionally attractive. He was, let's say, a little less sought after. Sometimes, I would joke and cruelly tell him I was doing my social service for the month by sleeping with an awkward engineer like him. Eventually, we fell in love. I apologised profusely to him for that jibe, and for not coming around to dating him sooner.

Over the next year, Hari and I had lots of arguments about politics—and lots of sex. Hari didn't really like condoms, so I went by myself to a gynaecologist for the pill and the lecture that comes free with it. There was nothing especially tender or thoughtful about sex with Hari, but it was all right. I remembered the things he told me he liked, and pretended to get just a little more excited than I actually was when he tried his newest moves. None of his newest moves included mastering the clitoris. 'I think you should do this yourself,' he would say, after a few minutes of prodding about. 'Don't worry about it,' I'd respond with a smile. Unfazed, Hari would continue heroically to the main event. After he had had his orgasm, he would ask me breathlessly, 'Did you?' Sometimes I would say yes, sometimes I would say no. Either way, Hari would kiss me, then roll off me and fall asleep. The point of sex isn't the orgasm anyway, I would tell myself, and fall asleep too, a little while later. Eventually, I just started saying yes when he asked. He did ask every time, though. That was thoughtful.

The years went by, we moved in together and Hari started to become less interested in sex. That's normal as a relationship goes on, I thought. Maybe Hari just can't keep up with me and I have unrealistic expectations, I thought. When I tried to bring it up, he said talking about how it made him feel emasculated and said dolefully that he could never make me happy. Sometimes, he said it was not me, that he just felt too lazy, had watched too much 'fucked-up' porn or had trouble with his body image. I felt guilty for pushing him and told him how handsome and attractive I thought he was. I bought nice lingerie and got really fit. But I noticed his disinterest was especially evident when I tried to initiate sex. Not when he wanted it, though. He got sad if I said I was tired, so I decided I was not that tired after all. Wasn't I the one harping on about how little sex we were having?

By this time, we only had sex when Hari decided we would. In moments of anger, I would try to tell him how I felt I had no sexual agency or control over my body, but feminist jargon had never been the way to Hari's heart. He would roll his eyes, then hug me and promise to make it better when I cried. If I said I was sad that maybe he didn't want me anymore, he would show me how much he did by tossing me around the room. 'I wonder if this is what being raped feels like,' I once found myself thinking casually, before chastising myself for being insensitive to people who really do get raped. One day, in one of these displays of masculinity, Hari called me a slut.

I froze for a second, but didn't want to ruin the mood. Later, while we were watching *The Handmaid's Tale*, I paused the episode. 'Hey, do you think maybe you can avoid that word you used yesterday? I don't particularly like it.' He said, 'It was just something I said during sex, you're impossible to please. Okay fine, I won't say it.' I gave him a kiss and hit play again.

Eventually, Hari decided we were to have sex mainly while I was asleep. The first few times, I thought it was kind of sexy. The next few times, I realised I really just wanted to go back to bed. One night, I thought maybe if I appeared to still be asleep, he'd get the hint. When he didn't, I let him get on with his business, to spare his feelings, while hoping he would be done soon so I could go back to the nice dream I had been having. In the morning, I wondered why I felt sort of sick inside. I decided to do what I usually do when I have awkward questions, and Googled, 'Did my boyfriend rape me last night?' The answers were inconclusive, but a bunch of self-help forums told me I should just tell him frankly how I had felt. That evening, I was especially quiet when we were both home after work, and Hari noticed something was up.

'Are you sad again? Is it about sex?'

'Um. Okay, don't get mad, I'm not saying anything drastic, but I sort of feel like maybe you didn't … I guess, what I mean is that I think maybe you didn't exactly have my consent last night.'

'Oh.'

'Look, I know you were really sleepy, we both were, but I guess I just didn't feel very good about it when I woke up.'

'Oh, well, I'm so sorry I made you feel that way. What are we eating for dinner?'

'Hm. Do you maybe want to talk about this some more?'

'But I said I was sorry, I was also really tired, I won't do it again, obviously.'

'Yeah, sorry, but I feel really upset and confused about what happened.'

'God, stop making me feel like a rapist, man.'

'Okay, okay yeah, you're right, never mind. Let's order something nice?'

Hari and I dated for a few more months after that. In that time, we had plenty of sex while I was asleep. Sometimes, I had to say 'stop it' a few times before he would listen. Sometimes, I got up and went away to pee and waited till he was asleep before I lay down again. Sometimes, I said nothing at all and let him finish. The night before he broke up with me, I was woken up for sex. He softly called me a slut, one last time. I didn't fight it; plus, I was the one who had wanted us to have more sex.

After all, sex is something nice two people do when they love each other.

4. Firefighting

UBON
Age Then: 26
Age Now: 31

This was shortly after I got married and my husband and I moved in together. We had very different work timings and I usually got home just around dinner time. He had a few hours free before and after dinner but worked till late in the night. One day, I came back home to find that he had made some spicy curry and rice. We ate it with great enthusiasm.

Since he had no client meetings later that night, we decided that it was time for some romance. Fortunately (but in this case, unfortunately), he likes to bring me to an orgasm first using his hands. As he started doing this, my nether regions started to burn. I ran out yelling and dumped a lot of water on myself. Then we realised that in an effort to be efficient and organised, my husband had cut up a whole bunch of green chilies to freeze that evening. Washing his hands twice with soap had not been sufficient to prevent my burning loins situation.

I think about this whenever I see a perfect sex scene in a movie because I know that sex in real life is often more interesting and much funnier than what we see in on screen.

5. A Kind of Boring One-Night Stand

ANONYMOUS

Sex can be so many things. It can be good, great, terrible, regrettable, hot and heavy, god fucking ugly, meaningful, not at all so, confusing. But this encounter is nothing like that. It was so normal that it took a while for me to make sense of it.

I always wanted to share this experience because of how unspecial it was, in a nice way. I started having sex with my first boyfriend when I was around sixteen (not an easy thing to accept by the way). He was a nice guy and we dated for four whole years. In time, things got bad, our paths changed and we became different people, accepted different distractions and ended up having a lot of bad, pathetic, gross, teenage sex.

I moved out of Calcutta, where everyone knows everyone, a small incestuous set-up. I had sex with a vengeance after that. I lost a bunch of weight, which made it easier to be woke (if you know you know), walked with confidence (only as much as Delhi can offer you) and without waxing my legs.

I ended up meeting a lot of nice people—interesting, ambitious, creative, etc. So, here is the thing, sex is always so loaded. It means so many things, and it somehow comes with these swiftly changing codes and norms based on reactions and observations. I realised that nothing was sacred and neither were the dumbass values that I had in my mind, which changes every day. The nuances keep shifting and building through this beautiful and exciting process of sex.

I have been lucky enough (though this should be normal) to have at no point of time 'had' to have sex. If I ever didn't feel like it, I didn't do it. But a good one night stand has left me confused, in agony or in a strange mood of self-hate and introspection … quite a few times.

But you get to know a thing or two about the usual set-ups when sex is a possibility. I went to a bar one day, without the intent of picking someone up, being picked up or pretending to be picked up. I went with a few of my friends from college and some other guy. Some Other Guy, the tag-along, was extremely good company. We talked over the music, not the typical 'singled out, let's go to a corner and talk about whatever the fuck you think the other one is interested in'—our discussion was dynamic and snappy. And then someone called us over to their house to continue the merrymaking.

A few failed attempts at drinking games later we all decided to play a song we really like. I played *Marinade*. Not a lot of people know that song but guess what, Some Other Guy did! We sort of looked at each other and thought 'Kindred souls!' (read: potential lay for tonight).

People got drunker and the songs got sadder, and a friend went on a Tinder date at 3 a.m. and everything made sense and it felt really nice. Some Other Guy asked if I want to go back to his place. I blamed convenience because he lived close to campus and had a spare mattress. The prospect of not having to go anywhere alone in Delhi at night overwhelmed me with gratitude. I agreed.

As we awkwardly waited for the cab to come, we discussed our favourite brands of cigarette (Benson versus Classic Regular, psht!). The Uber ride was overbearingly silent, and I sat still, haunted by the ghosts of my previous hook-ups. His place was tidy and minimal, decorated with film posters of shit made by Fassbender, Ozu, Ismail Rodrigues.

What if my breath smells, what if his smells, what if his dick is crooked to the left, what if he wants me to play dead, what if he doesn't have protection, should I leave right after or stay for breakfast?

But there I was with a beer in my hand, just looking at film posters.

Some Other Guy asked me to wait in the hall. I sat, contemplating the loaded nature of modern-day casual sex. *Fuck, what if I fall in love with him tomorrow? What if he does? Shit, shit!* I was sure that in the next few moments, I was going to see a naked guy, wearing only his socks, standing in front of me with his hands on his waist. People do that shit a lot. But then he reappeared with a laptop, still fully clothed.

I was shocked. Apparently all he'd thought about in the Uber ride was all the cool videos he'd wanted me to watch. He made me coffee so I could sober up a bit for the non-adult entertainment segment of this show. Oddly, I felt so happy. I totally wanted to do it, the word for the feeling would be 'chill'. I felt really chill about the situation.

We laughed and laughed and cried from laughing. We smoked a beautiful joint and went to the terrace for the sunrise. It took too long, so we came back and laughed some more. He asked if he could kiss me and I said something completely stupid that conjured up a bunch of crickets so I proceeded to kiss him first. It was a very good kiss. He asked me if I wanted to go ahead with it, and again, I said something completely awkward (read: *main toh kabse hu ready taiyyar*). We did it and we laughed and we got confused and fumbled, we moaned and gasped, and I came and so did he.

Then we talked while dramatically smoking some cigarettes like we were in a Godard film. Some Other Guy confessed that he also felt the pressure like me and he didn't know how to go about it. The consensus was that we were not going anywhere with this, it was all about the present and we would go our different ways without feeling burdened, hurt or sad. The only thing we'd have in common was *Marinade* and the hangover we would wake up to. He slept. I went to the bathroom, saw my reflection and didn't feel a thing. Not a single thought.

I woke up to some strange sounds. He was in his kitchen.

'Get me my coffee, bitch,' I said.

'On it. What do you want for lunch?'

'A quickie,' I joked.

He laughed at my terrible sense of humour, as well as determination. I said I had to go and he agreed. We hugged, added each other on Facebook and let ourselves be.

I had sex. It felt really good, and it wasn't all of those other things sex used to mean to me. This sex meant nothing, not that bad nothing (with the exclamation mark) but the *nothing* nothing—and that was the best part. I don't go about looking for that in general. It happened and could happen again ... or perhaps it would not. All these possibilities restored a certain faith.

Sex for sex, not for intimacy, vengeance, procreation, anger, horniness (okay, maybe a little), violence, love, friendship, nothing. It was two consenting, aware, well-adjusted (well, sort of) adults. That's my sex story. Boring sex rocks!

6. Is This Love That I'm Feeling (In My Loins)?

ANONYMOUS

Age Then: 21
Age Now: 27

I had recently had sex with my boyfriend for the first time. While I was never a prude and had engaged in other kinds of sexual intimacy, penile–vaginal intercourse had not yet happened. When I was twenty-one and in B-school, he came to visit me in my city (we were in a long-distance relationship). We booked a hotel and spent three days going at it like bunnies. Soon after, he turned emotionally abusive. However, this story is not about that.

A fellow student, who had more or less ignored me for three months, suddenly developed an interest in me. And before I knew it, we were sending each other text messages in class and coordinating when to bunk so we could fornicate in our hostel rooms. One look from him could set me on fire. He was the first person with whom I had multiple orgasms. He was the first person I had met who thoroughly enjoyed going down on women. He also helped me discover my sexuality by teaching me about my own body.

While all the sex with him has been great, the one incident that sticks out is this. He walked into my room with no warning. Locked the door behind him. Asked me to take my pants off. And went down on me like I was his sole source of nourishment and he was famished. I was moaning into a pillow because our hostel walls were thin. That was the first time I had multiple orgasms, maybe about four. He then got up. Looked at me. Smirked. Said, 'Thank you for dinner,' and walked out of my room. He never took his clothes off. He didn't expect any pleasure in return. It was that simple. It's been six years since we first had sex. The fire I feel in my loins when he is around is still the same. We have fallen in and out of love with many other people, but our sexual chemistry stays strong. I can be in love with the most amazing person in the world. But my body will always crave his.

❦

7. Raw Onions and the Moon

BRISHTI

Age Then: 21
Age Now: 22

The first time we kissed, we were both drunk on *bangla* (local alcohol you get in Kolkata) and ate raw onion with it. It was the best, most disgusting first kiss ever.

Another time, we were having sex in her bed. She was seeing another dude at that time and she would talk to me about him. He was a misogynist asshole, the kind your body is instantly attracted to while your mind screams at you to stay the fuck away. One of those fuckboys.

But she would talk to me about him in bed and that was fun. She was on top, and she asked me if she could show me something he does to her that drives her crazy. I said yes. She proceeded to hold my neck, choke me gently and tilt my head back. It was incredible. I felt super turned on, as though a light had gone off somewhere in my head. I had never been choked before, and since then, I haven't had sex where I haven't asked to be choked. It was amazing.

I remember going down on her, tasting her and being very surprised because her thigh tasted sweet! I couldn't stop biting it. Later, we hung out naked in her balcony under the moonlight/streetlights. It was great.

8. Liberated by Sex, Unexpectedly

JENNIFER
Age Then: 38
Age Now: 42

I had only a couple of dating experiences as teenager, but then I had an arranged marriage at twenty-two, and no sexual experience before that. I didn't know what to expect other than I liked kissing my past boyfriend. My husband didn't like kissing and due to my lack of sexual prowess, I didn't even recognise for years that he had erectile dysfunction at his ripe old age of twenty-six. I made do with oral sex and no intimacy but had two children by some miracle. The marriage was sexless and boring. He didn't want to find a fix. I knew in my heart that it was over.

I ventured into the world of online dating and found a man. He was younger by three years, divorced, with no children. I felt drawn to him, but not due to looks.

He was a stranger, we'd exchanged fake names. We met up, watched a musical and then went to his place. As things heated up, I resisted it a bit but landed up enjoying the oral sex and then the real deal. I was thirty-six and had been married for fourteen years. His long penis inside me, hard and deep, was the first time I understood what my body had been missing.

It was easy to fall in love with a stranger with the hormones that surged after he came inside me (yes, that's dangerous but I was not ovulating and really wanted to experience it). The warmth I felt was something else. Then the hormones calmed down, and I recognised we had little in common. But I did have encounters with him again and again. There was this one time, overlooking the river from his apartment, lying down after sex on top, his penis still inside me, the skies dusky. It was so awesome to have experienced it. I felt sexually alive, with each part of my body feeling gratified, touched and satisfied. I had no regrets, for in that moment, I came to a decision: whether I found another partner or not, it was time to walk out of my sexless marriage. And it has been the right decision.

9. Intimate from the Get-Go!

KARMASUTRA
Age Then: 25
Age Now: 25

I knew it was going to happen a long time before it did. I just hadn't zeroed in on when, but I think he had picked his opportunity well. He knew I would say yes, I thought I would not. He came prepared. We got to talking, and a frisson of electricity crackled between us. I knew I had lost. But it also felt like I won. I'd wanted him the minute I laid eyes on him that evening. At least he didn't know that.

He wasted no time in grabbing my waist and pulling me into a kiss; it was so quick that it caught me off guard. His audacity shocked me. Within a few seconds though, I was moulding my body against his to return his kiss. He was eager to remove my clothes, I was equally eager to undress him. In a flurry of seconds, we were both naked, and I was on top, never breaking our kiss for too long. We took turns taking charge, but suddenly he flipped me on my back. I trusted him completely, he made me feel safe. He smiled at me and put his fingers inside me. In just a matter of seconds, I had started moaning. The sensation of an unbridled orgasm was new.

He watched me hungrily, intent on my pleasure, kissing me as if he needed it to live. I felt worshipped. I entered realms of pleasure I had only read about so far in trashy books. It was overwhelming. Intense, yet fun. Passionate, yet gentle. Jumping into bed without building intimacy is rarely a good idea, but this was intimate from the get-go. Lucky me.

My next orgasm came, and he kept kissing me, murmuring words of comfort. I could feel myself loosening up from within. It was as if I had been repressed all my life. My third orgasm came, and this time, I saw genuine enjoyment on his face. Never before had a guy cared for my pleasure. By the end of this dreamlike night, my legs had turned to jelly. I was sore from all his ministrations.

I was all too aware that it may never happen again, but who cares? I had finally experienced the mythical multiple orgasms. It was amongst the best encounters of my life, and it forever changed my idea of sex. I no longer think that it is about control or letting go of control. It's about relaxing into your partner, and learning to accept every bit of your wonderful self.

10. Compartmentalised

LISA

Age Then: 37
Age Now: 38

I walked out of a dispassionate and manipulative twelve-year marriage and found myself right in the middle of a bitter divorce. Fuelled by long-standing craving for all things intimate and maybe some love, I led myself, eyes wide open, into a functional relationship, where the driving function is sex and a partnership to explore its different forms. The relationship filled the void of several years of no sex, but it did nothing to help experience the feeling of being loved. For three years, I struggled to keep the emotion of love at bay and not wait for reciprocation. I worked at understanding the concept of compartmentalising emotions, though I feared I wasn't capable of it.

Last year, our explorations led us to begin swinging as a couple. I had opened up enough to talk to my partner about being bi-curious. The first couple we met, the girl and I hit it off pretty well. We connected within the first few minutes of meeting, and I found that I was a natural at flirting with a woman. On the way back home, we couldn't keep our hands off each other, and by the time we got home, the men were ignored. That night, we had sex with each other's partners, as a group and eventually just the both of us. When she and I made love, she whispered into my ear that she loves me and asked if I felt same. That has remained etched in my memory, for I could not say it back to her, because that night I had realised I had just compartmentalised an emotion. Because all I said in response to her was, 'I know.'

11. Letting Go of a 'Great Guy'

AHENBLA
Age Then: 16
Age Now: 25

I was sixteen when I got into a relationship with a boy I liked, from my school in Delhi. I felt like I was in love, and that he loved me too. Soon after, while I was still under eighteen, he persuaded me to have sex with him. I agreed. It was consensual. What followed for the next five years, however, was not. Essentially in a long-distance relationship, he visited once every few months. During those times, he forced himself on me, forced me to indulge in sexual activities in public, forced himself on me on the street, commented on the kind of clothes I wore, got angry when I said, 'No, I do not want to have sex,' went off his rocker when I interacted with other men, ridiculed me by saying I had no male friends, and introduced me to his mother, who body-shamed me. One of the times we had sex, he clicked pictures of me and filmed me WITHOUT my consent. He told me about this only when, around five years later, I broke up with him. He threatened to misuse the pictures and videos, threatened to come to Delhi and/or send people to my address to fix me, wrote me a nasty email comparing me to rotten fish, whores, sluts, and accused me of being a terrible daughter who had no sense of 'compromising for the family'. This torture only stopped when I threatened to go to the police and his parents with the email he had written to me. For years, I lived in fear, blaming myself for not speaking out, for not talking about it to my friends or family, for not exiting such a toxic relationship. It was only recently that I managed to open up about this abuse to my best friends. When we broke it off, our mutual friends from school questioned me, persuaded me to get back with him, blamed me for not understanding him and for letting go of such a great guy. The most ridiculous bit was feeling the need to explain myself. Not a day passes when I don't shudder thinking about everything he subjected me to, while he saunters about in his circle of friends, pretending to be the good guy. We don't talk now. We're not in touch. But I deserve to live my life peacefully, without being afraid of sexual intimacy, with men who respect me. And this is my closure.

12. The Ghost of Aziz Ansari

YO TAMBIEN
Age Then: 20
Age Now: 23

We met on Tinder, and, after talking for a few weeks, spent a night together in a hotel. Neither of us had discussed our expectations for the night, or what we thought our relationship was.

We were drinking, sitting on the same bed. I did feel attracted to him but was also unsure—I'd never quite been in a situation like this. And then he kissed me. I kissed him back. He tugged at my shirt and took it off. I remember feeling vaguely uncomfortable. I wasn't a virgin, nor was I a stranger to hook-ups, but it just felt as if things were going too fast. I asked him to slow down, and we did.

The rest of the night is blurred in my head, but it went like this: we kissed some more, he took my pants off, then I put them back on. Then he seemed very disappointed, almost impatient with me for not being able to make up my mind. Suddenly, I was scared and confused. I was in a room with a guy I didn't know at all, and I had nowhere else to go. I had already kissed him, expressed some sort of sexual interest in him. He didn't force me into anything, but for some reason, I felt that by kissing him in a hotel room, I was expected to go ahead. So I did. We kissed again, this time I took my pants off and didn't put them back on. We slept together and it was all right—he was a nice guy but it wasn't earth-shattering. The entire time, this voice in the back of my head was telling me that this wasn't okay and I just wanted it to finish soon. Outwardly, I was enthusiastic, almost afraid to show him how hesitant I was.

I've thought about this a lot, especially since the Aziz Ansari story came out. In my case, I don't blame him exactly—he was not as persistent as Ansari. But it pains me that I was so conditioned that I thought I had no option but to sleep with him. It pains me that I didn't feel comfortable saying, 'No, let's just cuddle.' The fear that I was possibly being assaulted and forced to sleep with him propelled me to do it anyway, with fake enthusiasm: at least this way, I could control the narrative.

I often ask myself why I felt like I had no other choice, and I don't really have an answer. But perhaps it's because I knew that no one would be sympathetic to my circumstances. *You chose to go to a hotel with him—what did you expect?*

On another note ... I continued to see this guy. Many months later, we met up again in another hotel room. This time, we had sex once, after which I wasn't really in the mood and put off his advances. And he was irritated—angry, even! But I was more confident now and told him I didn't feel like it.

In fact, he was pushier the second time, but I held my ground. I refused to let him make me feel bad about saying no. While he didn't physically force me to do anything, there was something very discomfiting about the way he kept on making jabs at my refusal to have sex. I think men should be more mindful of that—it isn't only about physical compulsion, but about the subtle belittling that occurs when women don't do what men expect them to. Of course, that isn't confined to the bedroom.

That was the last time we saw each other. While it took me a while to put my finger on what exactly bothered me about our encounters, I feel like I've become far more confident about saying no. I'm proud to say that since then, I've only had completely consensual and generally excellent sex.

I sent him the article about Aziz Ansari and told him it would be good for him to read it. He responded with the *NYT* article that spoke about Aziz Ansari only being guilty of not being a mind reader. I suppose only one of us learnt from that experience.

The Woman in the Closet

ANSHUMAAN SATHE

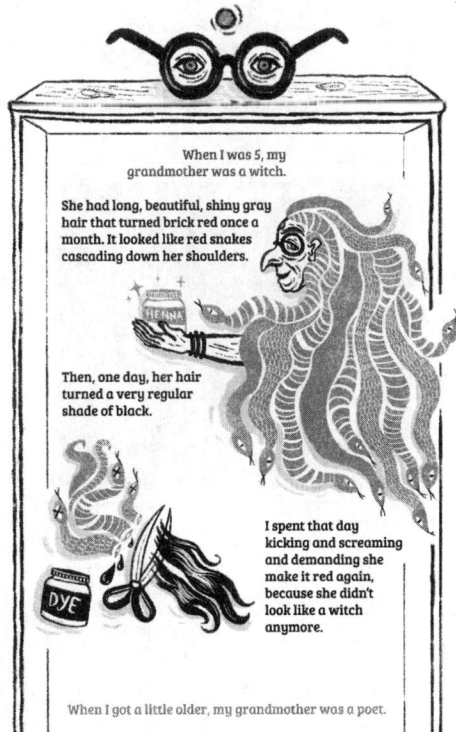

She had yellowed stacks of paper on which she wrote her poems. These poems were always about me.

Amazed that my antics were the source of such inspiration, I resolved to wreak even more havoc in the house so she would never run out of things to write about.

*"Lord my God, for what sin am I being punished? Why has this headache latched itself onto my sari?"

When I was 12, my grandmother was 69, and my mortal enemy.

She taught maths, and I hated maths, and our differences were irreconcilable.

I tore out pages of her prized books and broke all of her chalk in a fit of righteous rage.

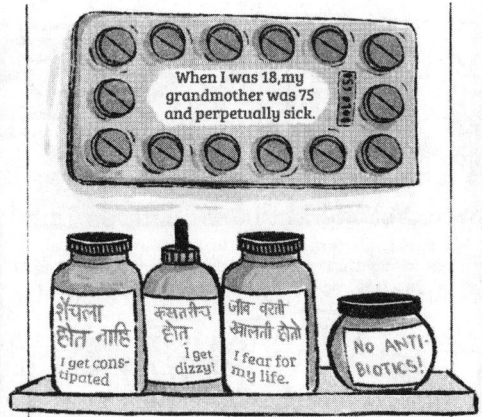

When I was 18, my grandmother was 75 and perpetually sick.

I get constipated. I get dizzy! I fear for my life. NO ANTI-BIOTICS!

Famously nit-picky about the medicine she was willing to take, she developed a reputation as the world's most accomplished hypochondriac.

When I was 21, my grandmother, was no more.

Now I am 22. I wish I could have seen her more clearly.

Growing up, I shared a room with Ajji. Our house was pretty small and cramped, and I complained that I needed my own space.

I complained about her old woman habits —

Why must you turn on the tubelight at 12 pm when it is so bright?!

Why do you need to be so noisy when you wake up at night to go do susu - thrice?

I told her to go live with my aunt if my messy chadar bothered her that much. But I never meant it – not really.

Despite what an outsider might make of our squabbling and complaining, it was how we loved and cherished each other.

*Give me that sheet you little brat!

*Take it na then, when did I stop you?

If Ajji were alive today, she would look at me with the same disdain she always did.

*Call yourself an artist? Where's your aesthetics when you leave your sheets in an ugly mess huh?

When Ajji passed away, we sat at my aunt's house sorting out her things.

Months after she is gone, we are still unable to tame the barrage of cupboards and boxes and trunks and suitcases in which she stored her life. Her objects, like her red hair, refuse to be tamed.

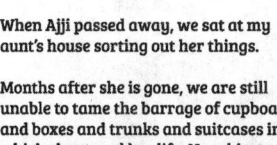

She lingers on in her plastic bags stuffed into Tupperware boxes that are stuffed into even larger Tupperware boxes,

in her old cotton saris that she refused to throw away because the cloth might be useful someday,

in her 3 identical pairs of bifocal chashmas because

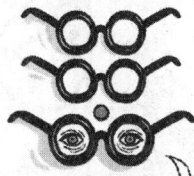

THEY Are for different chores, they make me see things differently.

Everyone in my family agrees I knew her best.

"Ajji, tell me a story na!"

आजजी मला गेष्ट सांग ना!

As someone who spent 21 years of their life being roommates with their 70 year old Ajji, I agreed too.

I never considered that my ajji was not always my ajji.

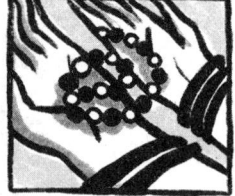

There are vast parts of her that I don't know, and this bothers me because it doesn't fit with my selfish fantasy of me being her closest confidant.

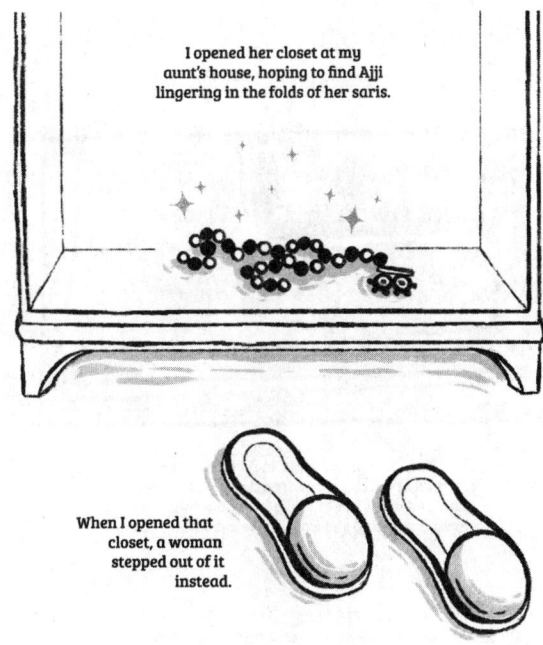

I opened her closet at my aunt's house, hoping to find Ajji lingering in the folds of her saris.

When I opened that closet, a woman stepped out of it instead.

In her closet, I found a little poem. It was about her own name. When she got married, her name was changed, as per custom, back then.

This is not news to me. In fact, I heard her talk about this a hundred times. But I never bothered to ask her how she felt about that - I never even considered she would have something to say.

Ajji would often angrily declare that "jithe ugta, tithe vikat nahi"- crops don't sell where they grow easily. Lengthy lectures about how she has touched so many people in her life, and how I am wasting her as a resource.

Am I your servant??

मी काय तुझी नोकर आहे??

WHO TOLD YOU TO CLEAN?

इंग्रजी मधे फाड-फाड बोलून दाखवू नकोस!!

Don't try to act smart in your English gobbledygook!!

As a child I looked at Ajji's closet as a wonderland of objects.

Her vast collection of poetry books, her ornate bird shaped hair clips, the ancient looking telephone diaries, the giant yellow geometry box and its equally giant blackboard.

अरे पसारा करु नकोस!!
Stop creating chaos!

Later, it just became a typical granny's closet in my mind, full of stuff.

Wonder is starting to return to me now.

I find the poems she wrote,

the memoir she started to write but never found the time to finish,

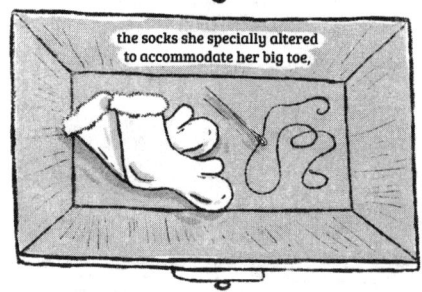

the socks she specially altered to accommodate her big toe,

her letters and photographs with childhood friends,

and I see a document of a life lived to the fullest by a woman who was so many things, and who was obscured by my vision of her as my Ajji.

Ajji would tell me I don't know how
to make friends. I would get furious –

"I have many friends, what do YOU know?!" I would say.

She would smile a very self-satisfied smile (irritating me even more) and say "Our understanding of the word friends is very different."

After her passing, I understood what she meant. The sheer volume of visitors surprised me.

It was a number befitting the 80 odd years of a life. Every person that came through the door spoke of her –

as a teacher, as a mentor,

as a sister, a child,

a young woman, as a friend.

And despite not having met some for years, I am sure Ajji would have greeted them all as friends.

To her, what makes friendships lasting is the ability to truly know a person, not just a part of them that is most relevant to you. It is the ability to look at someone and marvel at the big beautiful life they are leading.

Perhaps we all need 3 pairs of glasses to see the people around us differently.

After years and years of being around her, I am finally starting to be Ajji's friend.

Anshumaan is a graphic artist and illustrator based in Mumbai. They explore transness, the body and queer desire through art that is personal, playful and full of heart. They draw comics and can often be found by the sea. They wrote and illustrated this comic while working at Agents of Ishq.

YEARNING, SEARCHING, FINDING

I Dreamt of Having a Suhaag Raat Straight Out of the Movie *Kama Sutra*. My Actual Experience Was Nothing Like It

It's been a decade since I had sex with a man

RIMLI BHATTACHARYA

20 March 2018

It's been a decade since I had sex with a man. The last time I did was with my husband, whom I divorced.

As a young woman of eighteen, I watched the movie *Kama Sutra: A Tale of Love* directed by Mira Nair. *Kama Sutra* is a tale of love that also speaks about the art of love-making. I thought it would be considered taboo for me to watch this film, in the way that I had been cautioned not to read novels by Jackie Collins because she spoke openly about sex.

I came from a family of academicians. My parents were professors. My only focus had to be on studying: maths, science and, most importantly, moral science, an ICSE special subject on character building. So, by the standards of my parents and society, I shouldn't have been watching *Kama Sutra* at all. Rather, I should have been watching *Jhansi Ki Rani*, *Robin Hood* or *Jai Santoshi Maa*.

At eighteen I was intrigued by the name 'Kama Sutra' itself, and decided to watch it so that I could learn to make love well when I got married. The movie started with Maya, a maid, and Tara, a princess, who were best friends and also rivals. While the princess Tara was tutored by Rasa Devi in the art of love-making, which she couldn't use to her advantage, the maid Maya embodied the art.

I am a classical dancer, and I too dance to narrate stories with the rhythm of my body. With each melody, my steps can decipher the language of love. I have sensual features and can turn a man on with my moves. In the movie, both Maya and Tara danced in front of the king, and I dance in front of an audience. Sometimes the audience may be children, sometimes adults, but it makes no difference to me.

Raj, the debauched king in the movie, needed sex but ultimately fell in love with Maya, as she had in her the intoxicating passion of her soul. I felt in tune with Maya, I felt I could caress and kiss the man who would be my husband, I would moan when I made love, feel the touches that a woman needs from a man, take in the scent that could send me to a heady dawn, until two souls became one, nestled in as close as two spirits can be.

At eighteen, I wanted to be in the arms of my man, who would caress my neck and touch my earlobes. I wanted to let him leave the love bites on my breast, my nails shredding his back, as I say that is love. I wanted to be that lover who everyone would want to love. But I wanted all this inside marriage, with a husband.

I thought I would like to drape myself in a sari and look like a bride on my wedding night, a red bindi on my forehead and flowers in my hair. That night, he would come, lift my chin and wrap me in his arms as I trembled. I would feel that I was Maya with my lover Jai Kumar, whose hands would caress my cheekbones, touching my lips with his and enter me in all the positions explained in the book and shown in the movie. He would lift me off my feet and carry me to the designated bed for that first night. He would undo my blouse, his hands on my legs, my back arching in anticipation, just like Maya's when Jai Kumar touched her breasts, knowing well where his fingers would reach. My head would press into the pillow as he entered me, the first moan escaping my lips.

Then, at twenty-two, I got married.

I asked my husband to watch *Kama Sutra* with me. He said he had no time for it, but he had time for his friends with whom he went with to the movies. He did bring blue films home and asked me to watch porn with him, but I no longer felt I was Maya and he Jai Kumar—rather, that I was a mistress of Raj, the king whom he could fuck but not love. I wanted to watch *Kama Sutra* again, I wanted to teach him how to love a woman. I didn't want to watch porn as I knew it spoke about intercourse, while what I wanted was love. He felt he was too intellectual, and he did not appreciate such stupidity in the name of sex.

Looking back, on the first night of my marriage, there was no sex at all. During the reception, I had tripped on some stairs and bruised myself. My legs hurt, but he paid no heed and went off to sleep. The very first night, I understood he was arrogant. I'd felt that earlier when we dated, but I was in a rush to get married and ignored his abusive nature. The next day, my friend called to ask how my first night had been. I was telling her made-up stuff based on scenes from *Kama Sutra* when my husband snatched the phone from me and slapped me hard. He didn't speak to me for the next three days. On our honeymoon, he was furious when I asked the hotel reception to give us a room suitable for a newly-married couple. Again, he stopped speaking to me. And after punishing me for three more days, he tried to have sex with me but it was a disaster.

I could never talk to him about sex. We stayed married for eleven long years, but only on paper. I spent five years with him and my life was a living hell. I attempted suicide twice. He got me pregnant. I was a young woman, and other men looked at me with eyes full of lust. But I felt like I was being used as a doormat, not treated as a woman to be loved. Although we had a love marriage, I left him like Maya—walking away for miles and miles till he could not find me anymore.

I watched *Kama Sutra* again, this time as a single woman who needs and wants to be loved. Sex unites bruised souls and can ignite love in a person who has been unloved for decades. It is a balm for wounds and scars that haven't healed. It can make a relationship stronger—for me, love is incomplete without sex.

I still search for my Jai Kumar, I dream of him, I dream of a house where we will make love, where he will kiss me passionately, where he will love me completely as a woman. But that is just a dream, not a reality.

In real life, I watch *Kama Sutra* alone and I am Rasa Devi, who can teach the art of love-making through my dances, my mudras, my emotions. I am Rasa Devi, not Maya anymore.

Rimli Bhattacharya has a degree in mechanical engineering and an MBA in supply chain management. Her writing has appeared in several magazines, engineering journals, blogs, the Times of India *and in the anthology* Book of Light. *She is also a trained Kathak and Odissi dancer. Rimli lives in Mumbai.*

We Met on Grindr. Now the Intimacy of the Sex We Had Makes it Hard For Me to Forget Him

Some loves are sexual, where emotion, body and connection become powerfully joined in the intimacy of sex more than anything else

COMPLEX CHARACTER

8 November 2017

It was 2013 when AD and I matched on Grindr. It was just another casual encounter that would start with asking each other about location, preferences and most importantly, for pictures. From the beginning, I have always used my own pictures. Even though I am discreet, many warn against using my real pictures. But then my logic is simple. The only people who would know I am on the app would be those who are on it themselves. *Bhagwan ki daya se* I'm quite decent-looking, so I do get a good response. I don't approach though, and only respond to those who approach me.

AD was in Mumbai for a limited time, interning at an office close to mine. We quickly moved from Grindr to WhatsApp, where we began a mesmerising *silsila* of voice notes and pictures on the phone. It was very romantic. He would often say things like, '*Mujhe toh tumhara nasha ho gaya hai* ...' (You intoxicate me, I'm under your spell) or 'I can't keep my hands off you.' (And he never did!)

Soon, the time came to take this offline. After about a week or ten days of exchanging audio notes and pictures, we finally decided to meet. I picked him up outside his office in Dadar.

We met—and kept meeting. I had never ever experienced this rush before in my life. He would finish work and just scoot over to my office. I would give him WiFi access and he would wait in one of the cabins at the reception of my massive office till I was done. I would wrap up as fast as I could, and we would dash off in my car to the romantic getaways of South Mumbai.

All the while as I drove, he wouldn't keep his hands off me. Not even when we got out of the car. Whether it was Marine Drive, where we sat listening to music and facing the sea, at Scandal Point, the Tata Garden in Breach Candy, a movie theatre, or the nondescript countryside-like precincts around RC Church, he would kiss me at the slightest opportunity, without making it awkward for others around us. He would steal those moments very skilfully.

One moment lingers in my mind. It must have been mid-June of 2013—the always erratic yet sometimes romantic rainy *mausam* of Mumbai. We were parked in the lane opposite the Tata Garden. We'd bought some shrikhand at Breach Candy. In the car, he asked me to smear a bit of it on my lips, and he proceeded to lick and eat it off my lips, very many times.

Often, we would have a snack at the reasonably priced Status restaurant and drive around some more before I dropped him off at Churchgate station so he could go to his aunt's place in North Mumbai. The hardest thing for both of us was this moment of seeing each other off.

A Whole New Meaning Of I'm So Into You: Anal Sex

But our courtship didn't just end at kisses. He meant to take it further. Full intercourse. Something I hadn't really done before. He's younger than I (twenty-five to my thirty-four) but far more street-smart, and he knew a lot more about sex than I ever did. Although he came to my big city from a small town, between puberty and adolescence he'd seen, heard and experienced several facets of sex, that were still unknown to me, early in his life.

Between the two of us, he was the quintessential 'top' and I was the 'bottom'—everything between us also was like a stereotypical 'boy-girl' relationship. He had wooed me into meeting him, and now, sleeping with him seemed like a natural extension of what we had between us. We'd become great friends who loved to spend time with each other outside the bedroom as well.

So, after almost a month of regular meetings, when the time finally came for anal sex, I felt I had to rise to the occasion (though he was the one who needed to be erect). I'd always imagined it would be painful—and it was. But I had a guy who took every care to not hurt me, and most importantly, a guy I actually wanted to have that kind of connection with.

It happened. He penetrated me. Finally, I had penetrative sex for the first time and climaxed the way I felt I should. It was a bittersweet experience. Bitter, because after all, it is every bit as real as a tool going up your arse, and sweet because of a mental and emotional frisson it gives you. If done slowly, correctly and regularly, one comes around to enjoying it.

He explained the importance of being clean externally and internally before trying it out. He also ensured that during foreplay, my opening was relaxed and ready to be penetrated, and he tried out different positions so that we could do it successfully. In every sense, he has been my sex mentor. He was the one who introduced me to a gel called Xylocaine that, when applied to the anus, makes it numb to pain.

He was also the first guy whom I enjoyed giving a blowjob to. His full lips made every kiss to every part of my body extremely stimulating and special, especially since I also experienced an emotional connection. He was smart enough to use protection, and both of us knew it was the right thing to do.

But everything wasn't as smooth as I'm making it sound. Since I had no prior experience with anal sex, the first time had its share of problems. The first and foremost is not being prepared for the penetration itself (mentally and physically). So initially, I couldn't let him, but we tried different positions. He was slow and sensitive, and finally it happened while we were sideways. The biggest issue is being clean from within because it could really lead to some unsavoury stains on the condom which can be a turn-off.

I was determined to get there out of a feeling of intimacy and intense connection. But now in hindsight, I think maybe that feeling wasn't mutual.

After that first time, we had intercourse like this exactly six times more, and I could feel his passion to penetrate me diminish each time. Much as I wanted to become his best bet in bed, little did I know that, for him, it was essentially and always about moving on.

After those few sexual encounters, we would only go till a certain point—of foreplay, like kissing, and having me go down on him. Then he'd retreat. He would put off going further each time, often saying he was not in the mood. Maybe that was already the death knell, I don't know, since typically in many gay male relationships, sex plays an important role.

While our sex life was in limbo, his affinity for erotic chats with other men, and fantasies of conquering new bubble butts started to irk me and make me feel inadequate. The one who had inadvertently led me into this new carnal game had now abandoned me with all my new cravings, which I felt only for him.

'Rim' Jhim Ghire Sawaan

The experience of being rimmed deeply—where your partner makes passionate love to your butt and gently opens you up (with fingers and tongue) for the final intercourse, the urge to give your partner the pleasure that gives him a full erection, and the great satisfaction of taking an act of sex to its final outcome (climaxing with penetration)—was to glimpse intimate paradise. To be without it felt like being left in the lurch, halfway to paradise.

Sure, I continued to get a lot of attention from others, but my heart and body were still set on him, perhaps more so because I felt this lethal combination of passionate attraction as well as a sense of betrayal, all mixed together with an inferiority complex, while he looked around for other partners (even if it was only on chats, as he claimed).

Dammit, *Kuch Kuch Hota Hai* ... still!

Even as all of this unfolded, we remained inseparable, and that was what led me into a spiral of ambiguity. We spent all our time together. We kissed, cuddled and practically lived with each other. We claimed to be each other's biggest priority, even as the wholesome sex had flown out of the window, taking my peace of mind along with it.

One night, I slyly checked his phone and came across chats where he said he wanted to rim a guy 'for at least an hour', marry another, and wanted to make one in particular 'his bitch'. It shook me. And also woke me up. We had a loud fight.

Then another time, on a drunken night, he admitted to meeting a guy who was so thin that he'd lifted him up and fucked him. He seemed to have little qualms about revealing this even as we continued to feel friction because there was no such action between us.

But we didn't want to let go of each other just yet, so we continued being together almost everywhere. After a while, though, it all became too complex for me. Yes, there was no sex, but we did have our share of kisses and cuddles and intimacy in bed. The PDA was over, but genuine concern for each other was and is still there. At the same time, him wanting to do things with others, the same things that I sought from him, drove me up the wall.

The relationship (if I can call it that) started to diminish after almost two years when he finally moved to another part of the city for a job. While we met much less, we still chatted every day. I 'tortured' him for not being physically interested in me, and kept badgering and nagging him about his interest in others. What really made me insecure, jealous and extremely terrified was the thought of him giving intimate pleasures to some fair slim twinkie, a PYT who I felt was laughing in my face, able to enjoy what I sought from this one man and couldn't have.

Interestingly though, by now, we had several common friends who were all on a WhatsApp group and met on regular outings, so we somehow still managed to speak to or text each other every day.

Sometimes, we think of sex and love as different, and maybe they are. But some loves are sexual, where emotion, body and connection become powerfully joined in the intimacy of sex more than anything else. It is an intoxication, a *nasha* that's hard to forget because it runs deep.

Today, we are in different countries and I still chat with him on WhatsApp. We are still part of that common friends group on our phones. And we follow each other on social media. But when we chat privately, it almost always turns into a bloodbath of words because I still cannot get over the fact that he's just not that much into me anymore.

He always ends our conversations by saying that I'm very attractive, that there's nothing wrong with me and any guy would love to have me, but it's just that he cannot do it more than a few times with anyone.

Nice try, I want to say to him!

Complex Character is the guy who chose commerce over arts. He now writes, sometimes gets paid for it. He loves to travel, but sadly, his job doesn't take him places.

This Is Who I Am: How I Found Myself in Kink

A young man discovers his submissive nature and learns to be himself through BDSM and kink

KEVIN

1 May 2016

I checked my ticket to make sure I was boarding the right train. When I finally got on, I smiled a little. I was going back with a lifetime of memories from an amazing weekend with some of my closest friends. Even when I think about my past, when I wasn't so happy and confident, my smile doesn't disappear. Once, I'd half-believed that my presence in this world was a mistake. Something about the world felt so very wrong; I couldn't put my finger on it, but it was there, like a splinter in my mind, driving me insane. But as this was the only world I had, I'd tried my best to fit in. I lived my life and accepted the usual social customs: going to school, getting a job, worshipping God and so on. But the journey of finding my own self has been long, frustrating—and rewarding.

In my teens, I discovered a world with no borders, no discrimination, one that didn't cost much to travel in—the Internet.

I'd heard from all my hormonal guy friends about the porn they'd watched and how it was so erotic that they masturbated just thinking about it. I wanted to give it a try. It didn't really arouse me, but I was ready to explore that world. I watched more erotic movies recommended by friends and classmates just to see how it felt first-hand. But each time I tried to masturbate, I grew tired and gave up.

For a while, I wondered if there was something wrong with me. But I was still hoping that if I pretended that I was just an average dude then maybe everything would be all right. In a way, without knowing what I was doing, I had begun to explore my own sexuality.

When I was sixteen, I got friendly with a guy in my class and ended up sleeping with him. It was the first ever relationship in my life. Over the next five years, whenever we slept together, I never wanted to be the top. I was really content being the bottom half of the relationship, the more submissive partner in every sense, not only physical.

Afterwards, I would find myself re-imagining the same situation but with a woman on top of me, fucking me with a phallus. Just the thought meant I went to sleep with a rock-hard erection. I still hadn't learnt the art of masturbating. And I was absolutely ignorant about BDSM.

When I was eighteen years old, I became very good friends with a girl. I had my first sense of how different a girl's life is from a boy's. I was also mostly ignorant on the feelings of love and care for a girl. If I try to define my feelings for her now, it was love, but I didn't realise it at that time. I just knew I was very happy whenever she was a part of my day. In many ways, she was the 'one' for me as I couldn't imagine what my life would have been like if I hadn't met her.

When we used to talk, there were quite a few instances where she made me say or do things I really didn't want to, or wouldn't have had the courage to do if she hadn't ordered me to. Like once I 'let slip' I liked a girl but was too scared to ask her out—which I really was. She instructed me ask her out. This gave me a surge of energy—and also the courage to ask the girl in question out. Another time, I was feeling terribly low and she commanded me to cheer up or she would break all ties with me. This immediately gave me a rush of energy. It stimulated me both erotically and emotionally. So much so that I tried (purposefully but covertly) to land myself in helpless or embarrassing situations in front of her. The sense of power she had over me turned me on immensely. She had no idea of my feelings, I think. After all, I also believed my feelings were brotherly for a while. When we were a little older and she became interested in other guys, I disliked it. But I didn't question anything. I was addicted to the miniscule adrenaline spikes I got from our relationship.

And it was around then that I first understood I had a submissive nature. It was an innocuous incident but holds a very special place in my heart. I was playing Charades with my brother, his friend and the friend's sister. I teamed up with her while my brother and his friend formed the opposing team.

The first movie I had to enact was *Joru Ka Gulaam*. I tried acting like Govinda. I tried other predictable gestures with my partner to get her to understand the movie title. All of a sudden I had an epiphany. I gestured to her to rise from the floor and sit on a chair. She got up, bewildered, but she did as I said. Then, I closed my eyes, thought of the stars and fantasised that she was my lover, and knelt down in front of her.

To the others, it presumably looked like a serious attempt to win my turn. They couldn't have guessed what a transcendent experience I was having!

The adrenaline, the skipped heartbeat and tears of joy that almost escaped my eyes all said the same thing to me: 'This is how I am made. This is who I am. This is what I am meant to be.'

These lines went through my head and my heart and got imprinted there. I'd no idea why my play acting made me feel like that or why it took me till this moment to realise this, but once I did, there was no turning back. I took a break after my turn and went to the balcony. My heart was far away, flying through the night sky. I had finally identified myself.

⁓

One day, I stumbled across literotica.com, where authors post erotic stories in many categories and genres. In the BDSM category, I clicked on a story by an author called Rita (name changed). It was a turning point in my life.

Rita's story opened up so many new possibilities. It was about a couple who wanted a 24/7 female submissive, written in such a beautiful yet accessible manner that even a novice could grasp the difference between a healthy, mutual, BDSM dynamic relationship and an unhealthy one.

I read all her stories one by one. Did people who like to surrender really exist? Or was it just the stuff of fiction? I'd always thought that people who get pleasure from having their will taken away, who enjoy being hurt physically by others belonged in one place: a mental asylum. I read Rita's stories again and wrote a line of appreciation underneath each. Soon, she replied, thanking me for my compliments. That was my first doorway into the world of kink.

At first our interaction was purely writer-and-fan but we eventually exchanged personal emails. Ever since the day I'd played that game of Charades and recognised my submissive nature, I'd been afraid to discuss with anyone. Talking with an author from the other side of the world seemed like the safest way to get my questions answered. She seemed nice, patient and knowledgeable. Later, I mustered the courage to ask her my questions. She answered with more questions that pushed me to think and also gave me a peek into her 24/7 BDSM lifestyle with her husband/Master. BDSM now seemed like a deep, blue ocean and not a tiny, shallow stream. I was really blessed to have a friend like her.

'Can you please move to your berth?'

The voice of a fellow passenger pulled me out of my memories. I climbed up to my berth to lie down for the night. I turned to my side, immediately winced and lay on my back instead. I smiled; the pain was such a sweet reminder of my magical weekend. I couldn't wait to look at the marks.

I remember then what was it like for me when I didn't know this feeling.

One day, Miss Rita and I thought it might be fun to have an online dom–sub play session. She sent me a lot of questions in advance—what I looked like, what I was looking for from the power play. I had to Google several terms—like 'OTK' (which is 'over the knee') and 'collared' before I could answer her questions honestly.

As she was a writer and I an aspiring one, our playing quickly escalated into a totally different world with no boundaries, where all our dreams came true. There were some things in the play that I loved, some that I liked and some that I disliked, but every scenario taught me something new. I constantly wished that this world was real.

Miss Rita introduced me to a kinky social network. When I joined it, I was transfixed by the sheer number of sub men in there! Almost too many to count!

I found an Indian kinky group within the site and at once felt that this was a place where I won't be judged or thought of as a weirdo. This feeling itself was like a treasure to me, where I could finally open up the big box of secrets locked inside my heart that I'd only shared with Miss Rita so far.

As I followed the discussions on the group boards avidly, I realised I didn't know anything about BDSM in real life. At first, I was a silent but keen observer. When I first saw a thread about real-life meetings in various Indian cities, I was really tempted. But the threads didn't reveal what actually happened at the meetings, and I couldn't find one in my city so I let fear take over. My biggest apprehension was whether these meetings with kinksters were safe. Gradually, I began to interact. I saw a post on the group by a guy who was looking for a mentor in the BDSM world. I posted a comment wishing him luck in his search. He thanked me via a private message. His name was Ashok (name changed). I learnt that he had attended a few meetings in Kolkata.

One day, when I was at work, Ashok sent me a message saying he was going to be near my town the next day. We could meet if I wanted to.

I was very nervous. I didn't know whether I wanted to meet a total stranger I knew from a kinky website (of course, not considering that I was also a stranger from a kinky site). Then I found a thread on the site about the dos and don'ts of meeting a new person for the first time in the real world. I read it and decided to follow the instructions to the letter.

I called Ashok and he told me to come to a hotel, but I declined as the rules said to always meet a new person in a public place. Instead, I suggested an overbridge near his hotel. I laugh now on my choice of a 'public place'. I was indeed very nervous.

Ashok turned out to be a calm and knowledgeable person with a soothing voice. I asked him all my questions and told him that I'd once had a relationship with a man—something I'd never shared with anyone. He was nonchalant and understanding. He applauded my courage to think about my own nature as a submissive. He said he was new to the kinky lifestyle but he knew people who were experienced.

I asked him about the meetings and he said it was no different than getting coffee with a group of 'regular' friends. And, in fact, a month or so after I met Ashok, I had the chance to go to Kolkata to attend my very first real group meeting.

As I sat there, watching other people at the same table talking about kink as lightly and enthusiastically as though they were talking about cricket, I was amazed, even overjoyed by their attitude and zeal for kinky lifestyles.

At the meetings, I learnt men can be submissive, women can be dominant, some can be both. Being kinky is not an illness, nor is it a mental instability or a result of an improper childhood. It was simply a choice for some, a way of life for others, and for some, merely something to spice up their bedroom life.

I listened closely, asking questions from time to time. For the first time ever, I felt like I was doing something for me. The desire to learn more brought me back to the group again and again. Later, I pitched in to help organise events in Kolkata that the group hosted, and in the process, I made some wonderful friends. I had finally found people I identified with, who loved me for who I am and not what I can pretend to be. It had been incredibly hard to find.

≈

I can't remember when I had drifted off to sleep in this rocking train. I open my eyes and think. My own past self would hardly recognise me now. I have learnt that being submissive by nature doesn't mean that I had to be a pushover in everyday life. I can still be fierce at my job, be affirmative at home and loud with my friends!

I live a 'normal life'. Most people around me have not a clue how extraordinary my life is! I end my story with a favourite quote, 'Life is not just about who you are, what matters more is how you live it.'

Kevin is a submissive who became aware of his kinky side in 2008 and has never looked back since. He is a member of The Kinky Collective, which shares his vision to make 'kink' a friendly word in the Indian community.

Jeep Mein Beep, Dil Mein Dhak

He winked at me in the rear-view mirror and I was overcome with shyness

KAVITA DEVI BUNDELKHANDI

5 August 2016

At first, when I started to write this story, I thought I would choose another name. I chose the name used by Sridevi's character in the film, Chandni, meaning moonlight. That romance, her blue chiffon sari, the looking into each other's eyes. I thought it suited my love story, of which I am the romantic heroine.

But, well, my name is Kavita, meaning poem. And this is my story of true romance. I'm from Bundelkhand. I had joined a women's organisation where I had learnt to read and write, and soon became a journalist for *Khabar Lahariya*, a newspaper run by women, mostly Dalit.

Once, the organisation ran a campaign that required us to travel through the region for a few days. We had hired a jeep for this. So there we were in a vehicle, some women, some men and, in our midst, the beautiful driver—tall, fair-complexioned, with hazel eyes. The moment I saw him, our eyes locked. No one could accuse him of being shy. Wherever I sat in the jeep, he would adjust the rear-view mirror so our eyes would meet. Again and again and again. I would gaze at his face, and he would look at mine. I tried to avoid looking, but I just couldn't resist sneaking a glance.

Then one day, he looked at me boldly, and winked in the mirror. I felt a jolt. I was bashful, I was melting. From that moment, a restlessness took hold of me. I was in a fever; there was no peace in the day nor sleep at night. Always with people, no words could pass between us. But we were both drenched with the same thoughts.

One night we were all staying in a dormitory—sleeping in a row in a big hall. The thought that he was not far thrummed through me. In the morning, as I was going downstairs, I encountered him. We looked at each other. He grabbed my hand. My body felt rooted to the spot. Panicked, I pulled my hand away and ran off, almost tripping. I stood somewhere catching my breath, electrified, buzzing and terrified that someone might have seen us. I kept thinking about it, and every time I remembered his touch, I descended into a kind of *sukoon*, a cool, dark calm.

The next day, when I opened my bag to take out a pen, I found something inside. It was a note. It said, 'I love you, Kavita. I don't think I can live without you now. Say you feel the same. You have to say yes!' I read that note twenty-five times. When he had touched my hand, I'd felt electrified, but reading 'I love you' was twenty-five times more electric.

I would read those words over and over, through the day and until I drifted to sleep at night.

At that time, he had a phone. I didn't. That letter was the only link between us because we lived far apart. And there was a real fear of social repercussions in our villages. That fear was real and complicated. Because here is the thing: I wasn't a young, single girl entering some new, innocent love story. He was married, and so was I. We both had families and children. There was fear of dishonour, fear of slander, fear that someone might see us together and spread rumours.

But desire had found its way between us and it refused to leave. The only time I could read the letter was when I went out into the fields to relieve myself. There, squatting behind the bushes in a rare moment of privacy, I would read that letter over and over, thrilled at the words. My heart would beat so loudly in my ears, *dhak-dhak, dhak-dhak*, that I would look around to see if anyone could hear it. And then I'd hide the letter in my sari and return.

As the days went by, I began to worry—what if someone found the letter? What if someone checked my bag? So I soaked the letter in water, crushed it reluctantly and scattered the pieces in the field. I was bursting to express my feelings. To say, 'I love you too.' I was restless with desire.

Whenever I sat beside him during work trips, driving through those village roads, I would think about how beautiful he looked. I just wanted to touch him. But we were never alone. My heart was full, and I couldn't hold back anymore. I wrote 'I love you' on a tiny piece of paper and left it on the driver's seat. I watched from a distance; I was scared it might fall into someone else's hands. When he picked it up and read it, relief flooded me. Once he read it, I knew he understood that I accepted his love.

After that, the days passed listlessly. Now we both had said 'I love you', our hearts raced even faster. Food didn't taste good, sleep eluded me. Whenever we were in the same room, we would keep glancing at each other. We wanted to say so much, but just couldn't.

One morning, as I was washing up outside, he came up to me and said, 'Do you love me or not? Say something.' I did, deep inside, but I couldn't bring myself to say it. I felt all kinds of emotions but couldn't say a word. He said, 'I can't bear it anymore, I feel like just driving the jeep into a ditch!'

We both wanted each other, and we were both behaving crazily like people in a Bollywood film, uttering movie dialogues. It was that feeling of being in love, which is a trance, a dream, a song in a movie.

I had been married as a mere girl. This romance held a youth I had never had.

That night, he drove me home. On the way, he stopped the vehicle, hugged me tight and we kissed. Neither of us wanted to part, but we both had homes and families to return to. So we separated again, and our nights passed, both of us lonely and yearning, with only our letters for solace. I waited for many days for another work trip to happen so I could see him.

It finally came. We were in Chitrakoot for work. When we met, he only said, 'Meet me at the crossroads in ten minutes.' I knew I was crossing a border, going towards a place of no return. but I could not hold back. He was waiting for me in an autorickshaw. He pulled me in by the hand, and we drove, a bit intoxicated, to Ramghat, the riverside with its flower-bedecked boats.

On the banks of the river we talked and talked, about life. We swore to love one another forever. We made promises like only lovers can. Things back then were simpler, in some ways cheaper too. So we got a room in a lodge for fifty rupees and spent the night lost in joy, in pleasure, in adoration.

After that we simply decided that we would live together, no matter what the world thought, no matter what our families did. We moved in, and somehow despite its sharp scrutiny, the world slowly accepted the strength of our bond, and fourteen years have passed since that night, just like that, in love.

Living together, in our parts, might seem unthinkable. Society fills us with fear, makes us feel certain things are impossible. Love is a kind of crazy courage because of which you sometimes take a leap. And on the other side a new possibility, one you never could have imagined, comes to be.

Kavita Devi Bundelkhandi is the co-founder and editor-in-chief of Khabar Lahariya, *a rural news platform run entirely by local women journalists. This account first appeared on the Agents of Ishq podcast.*

Hyenas, Orangutans and Discovering My (A)Sexuality

The zebra does not concern itself with erotic fantasies

LONAV OJHA

27 February 2023

'Look at her tits, bro,' said my well-meaning classmate once in the social science hour.

'Eh,' I replied. 'They were much sexier before she decided to take her clothes off.'

He looked at me like I had violated the twelve sacred commandments of porn consumption, all at once. 'Kela, why would you say that? Look!'

I looked, and I looked more, and I'm sure even the teacher looked, but it wasn't until half a decade later that I understood what I should have much earlier.

I started my schooling by making everyone believe that Power Rangers were real. 'Listen to me, the Yellow Ranger stays here, at our school,' I told them. All they had to do was sneak into this vacant room on the third floor and he would be happy to hand out morphing gadgets. My classmates would begin arguing about which colour they get to be, and then I would feel super important and cool. Thankfully, nobody would be brave enough to creep into that room, and we would never find out who lived there (possibly the watchmen, or the sisters with their stern and soft and tired faces).

Once they'd grown some pubic hair, though, my classmates forgot my scam but would no longer be part of my bullshit. They ostracised me from *dhora-dhori*, a game where kids chased each other like Timon and Pumba. But I didn't think anyone in my class was cute enough to be called Timon and Pumba. I thought of them as the hyenas from *The Lion King* instead—the secondary antagonists.

The hyenas in class used to laugh with their stupid teeth when they were happy and cry with their stupid teeth when they were whacked by the fat stick that the teacher wielded. Years later, just before matriculation, two hyenas would elope to another state after having steamy sex on Teacher's Day, manifesting some kind of post-traumatic daddy disorder that definitely goes back to the caning.

I thought I was the same as the hyenas—I wouldn't mind running off from school with my partner—but something was off. This became more and more obvious with each passing grade.

The hyenas invested their energy in rubbing my face in the mud fields of Assam, stealing tiffins, and peeking over the urinal walls to check out the size of my dick and swat me in the balls for the next hour like some Spartan general testing out the limits of his soldier—only to lead the discussion towards girls and their pussies. I was still very preoccupied with jump-dancing in my room, slaying dragons, making pacts with wizards and charting landscapes filled with adventures, all while imagining someone I'd share my life and my adventures with.

Clearly, I wasn't partaking in the same erotic fantasies as the hyenas, even after growing older, even after starting to find the Power Rangers boring (the CGI had stopped looking realistic) and even after picking up emo boy stoic philosophy and self-help books that tend to fascinate emo boys of that age. Even as I thought that was a sign of growing up, the hyenas seemed to have skipped many levels and were more enthusiastic about Mia Khalifa and Johnny Sins. Most of them already planned to pursue science, expecting a fat salary and a hot wife who would keep them super happy like Yo Yo Honey Singh, whose songs were all the rage before Ed Sheeran came and made everyone fall in love with an anonymous person's body.

Degenerates like me took humanities. I expected a different crowd here, one filled with similar degenerates. Yet half a country away, far from home, nothing changed. Everyone still had a thing for everyone else. But it was here in Bangalore that I learnt the world isn't only filled with hyenas, that there is in fact a rather strong fauna diversity to gawk at.

Iguana, a self-established hopeless romantic in college, kept asking if I liked anyone. I kept saying no, but then she wouldn't believe me. 'How's that possible, bro?'

Cat would offer help. 'What if we set you up with someone? Like that *Community* episode where they try to get Abed a girlfriend until they realise Abed could get any hot girl he wants on his own.'

Raccoon said she knew someone in college with a crush on me. 'Nice,' I replied with a straight face.

'I used to fall in love every other second,' Orangutan said. 'I had once fallen in with Cat. I later learnt that she was in love with me too. She wrote a poem and published it in the school magazine under my name. But it was too late.'

In between cab rides and canteen food, Llama, who wouldn't date anyone shorter than her, asked, 'Are you sure you're straight?'

Questions, questions, and I had no answers. Until a Reddit meme showed me an incomplete keyword 'Asexuals are …' and Google suggested 'invading Denmark', 'gods' and 'coming for the iron throne'.

Like some of my friends who were allies before they figured out they were queer themselves, I didn't realise I was asexual until I began relating a little too hard with the memes. It led me to places such as r/aaaaaaaccccccce and the AVEN Wiki. The friendly spectrum-based nature of this new identity and its individually negotiated vocabulary not only gave me the dignity I deserved but also the freedom to think outside compulsory sexuality (the assumption that all people are sexual) tattooed on the body of our society, as well as its institutions and its people.

I have been in relationships before. The last one nurtured me, propelled me and seemed four years too short. I did also eventually like someone in Bangalore—a close friend of mine, Iguana—but it wasn't until I was head over heels for her that I felt attracted to her in any other way.

It's a funny time to be on the asexual spectrum in India. As a country that refuses to talk about sex, and is only beginning to accept romance, I'm surrounded by old people who will celebrate my 'celibacy' (provided I'm not of marriageable age yet) and sex-positive young people who will break their heads wondering how I can exhibit sexual inclinations despite being asexual.

It's also a funny time to be in the LGBTQ+ community. A bisexual friend of mine recently said, 'If you're asexual, how do you know you're not attracted to men?' He had had a crush on me for years, and suggested that I try going out with men to see if it worked. Or I could kiss him and find out. This is no different from what straight people tell gay people—how will you know you're not into girls if you haven't kissed them?

The ace community parachutes in with their memes. 'I think of attractive people like beautiful sunsets. I don't want to fuck a sunset.'

Maslow, in his triangular hierarchy of needs, very popular among psychology and business enthusiasts, had put sex at the base, along with food, shelter, air, food—the very things that keep us alive. In other words, sex must be an inextricable part of the human experience, and nothing could be more normal than wanting it bad, all the time.

The converse must also be true. When fans asked the showrunner of Sherlock Holmes if Sherlock is asexual, he said, 'There's no fun in that.' Predictably, most asexual characters on TV are aliens, robots or psychopaths. The few characters that are human are only implied and not canonically confirmed. This reminds me of the way heteronormative studios in the twentieth century coded gay characters by their dressing sense and mannerism to avoid referring to them as gay. The result being that the knowledge of asexuality and its agentic nature remains out of the mainstream, and people like me wouldn't find out that it's a thing until much later in their lives. Over the past decade, canonical gay and lesbian characters have multiplied incessantly, with Western studios trampling on each other to pursue their shiny and golden tokenism, but we await a film to explicitly mention asexuality.

It's no wonder then that I wanted to feel visible. I wanted someone, anyone to relate to. It used to make me sad. *Koisenu Futari* comes to mind. The plot is basic—what if two asexual-aromantic people start living together and call it a family? (And yes, they use the terms 'asexual' and 'aromantic'). Watching that one Japanese drama made me feel more seen and more heard than I had in my whole life, even though I'm not aromantic, even though I inhabit the opposite end of the spectrum. There was something odd and crippling about the loneliness of not fitting in, especially among people already fighting from the margins. The show and the online community made me realise that there are people like me everywhere, not as visible, maybe because it's not safe to come out, maybe because there aren't enough stories telling them what happens after, maybe because they don't know what it means. Maybe I could do something about it.

Growing up different in every way, asexual and autistic, fantasy bridged the divide between me and the reality that be, as my Power Ranger stories inspired, but it also did something else. It's given me purpose, hope and something to like about the world. It's given me enough, until I could see the world as more than hyenas, as sparkling, funny, compassionate people who dance and love and have sex in the most brilliant and weird ways, even if I'm not into it all the time or experience it differently.

It's given me the courage to question the essentialist assumptions of sexuality—that it's something inherent, unchanging and meant to be quantified and fit into neatly drawn boxes, that you're either heterosexual, homosexual, bisexual, asexual, or you're nothing at all.

Most importantly, it's given me stories to write about, and people who might read them.

Lonav Ojha is a zebra from Tezpur. He loves eating, staring at the ocean, hosting kitty parties and writing at Stories Under My Bed. On select afternoons, he saves the world.

My Male Friends and I Talked About Sex Constantly, But Not How We Really Felt About It

I'm trying to unlearn everything I'd absorbed in predominantly male spaces—it's making me a better person

SUDHAMSHU MITRA

13 November 2018

Lately, I have been going on dates using apps such as Tinder, Coffee Meets Bagel and OkCupid. I have been trying to understand how to navigate the dating space and the ways in which I can interact with the people I date. I am trying to reflect on how to practise kindness, empathy and honesty in the relationships that I build with them. Some of this has to do with having newfound knowledge and realisations about the world around me after completing a liberal arts course. In other words, when you start thinking about your actual life and actions in the light of the theory about rights, equality and power you are reading, you begin to ask yourself some searching questions. While it has been only a few months since I began, I have learnt a lot over this period. I have learnt how much I actually know (or rather, how much I don't know) about dating, sex and relationships.

During my days as an engineering student, my male friends and I talked about sex and about women constantly, but not in ways that were kind to us or them. These conversations involved sexist comments about women on our campus—how 'hot' a woman was, how 'bang-able' she was and fantasising about what it would like be to have sex with a particular woman. We would share pictures of 'hot' women with each other and comment on them. We would crack sexist jokes that involved caricaturing and objectifying the different body parts of a woman in many of our conversations and through doodles on our desks. 'Boobs' and 'ass' were words we used all the time. And there were conversations around masturbation, though predominantly expressed as jokes. We would talk about how many times we would have masturbated, the different ways in which we did it and shame the ones who did not know about it. Instead of saying, 'Get lost' or 'Go away,' we would say, 'Go masturbate,' ('*Hodko*', as it is said colloquially in Kannada).

The fact was that most of us hadn't had real sexual relationships with women (at least in my circle of around twenty men). But even among the ones who did, the conversations centred around the kind or number of blow jobs that one would have received, whether it was first or second or third base, if a particular porn position had been tried out, or how the woman had appreciated the size of one's penis. We'd talk about the porn videos that we watched, the best porn stars, the size (in gigabytes) of porn videos that we had or had just downloaded afresh.

But we never did talk honestly about sex and our emotions. We hit the bottle whenever we felt lonely or disappointed if rejected by a woman. We didn't have conversations around our ignorance and apprehensions on how to have sex; around our physical and emotional needs of being cared for, loved, validated and held; on the ways in which we could deal with our libidos instead of excessively consuming porn; on the ways of building a nurturing relationship and handling jealousy; or on the ways in which we could handle the breaking up of a relationship in a healthy manner.

This was also the time when many of us weren't being hugged, held and provided other forms of physical affection by our parents, who distanced themselves from us when we became adults. The only intimacy we as men could share was when we hung out together playing computer games, in bars, hanging out in college and attending concerts. If one did not have a girlfriend or wasn't dating, then one would be bereft of any physical affection. Any other forms of intimacy such as cuddling, hugging each other for long, holding hands, kisses were all sexualised, and our homophobia prevented us from being intimate. (We would make videos about 'gay' relationships with sexual undertones and post multiple Facebook statuses and comments laughing about how 'gay' someone is or how one is of the 'other' gender. All of this also meant that if there were times when I wanted to explore my sexuality with men, I would feel so overcome with guilt about just having these desires that I could never even allow myself to think about it, forget summoning the courage to talk about it with my friends.)

We could only cry in front of each other when we were completely drunk. After a year or so of being in college, most of us dealt with our loneliness, sadness, grief, heartbreak and anger predominantly by isolating ourselves in our rooms, crying, writing poetry or watching something to distract the mind. While we hung out together very often, we rarely opened up, touched each other affectionately or dealt with our thoughts and feelings honestly without the fear of being shamed, sexualised or laughed at. We did not know about the concept of patriarchal masculinity, that it had resulted in a loss of touch and intimacy. Neither did we discuss this loss with each other nor were we taught how to deal with it by our parents and relatives.

Right now, during the dates I go on, I can see the repercussions of growing up amidst a traditionally masculine space. It takes effort to identify the emotions I am going through at every point and then to deal with them in a healthy manner through constructive conversations. There is always an apprehension that I might do something to disappoint my date.

What if I'm not good at kissing? What if things go further, and I am not good in bed? Will my partner be okay with someone who is inexperienced, and still learning how to have sex? Is my inexperience going to be an impediment to having a relationship? These are things I feel fear and shame about.

Sometimes, it is difficult to understand whether or not I am using my date as a distraction from my other wants and confusing my need for love and affection for a need for sex. At times, it is hard to be truthful and say that I am not interested in a sexual experience, and other times, I am not sure how to articulate my interest in wanting to explore another body without alienating my date. But as I read about the #MeToo movement or different articles on feminism, I see so many of these experiences in a different light and the necessity to explore a new path ahead.

With such thoughts on my mind, my behaviour has changed. Every time I go on a date with a woman, when we are in a private space, there seems to be an unsaid pressure looming around on me—the pressure to 'make a move' or to 'make out'. It is, in fact, very hard for me to understand if my desire to kiss someone is genuine or if it comes from this unsaid pressure. I had always believed that the man should make the first move. 'What's a date without a little hanky-panky?' is a thought that I have always had to encounter. In one instance, I chose not to 'make a move' first. And because of that we spent a marvellous time together filled with conversations and a movie.

Once, I asked my date if she wanted to kiss, and she said yes. It felt liberating. While there is this notion that it is unsexy and ruins the moment to talk about these things before making out, I do believe that you can establish consent through conversations and, by being acutely aware of how the other person is responding to your move, still make it sexy and romantic. Now I have made it a rule of thumb to try my best to talk about my feelings before and after sex. While I'm still uncomfortable talking about things like loneliness, existential angst, sexual desire, my longing to be held, my few experiences of sex and my limited knowledge on different sexual positions, I have understood that talking about them enhances the experience I share with my dates.

Not making sex or heavy petting the central purpose in my relationships with my dates also opens up other forms of association that we may not generally get to experience. One of my relationships now involves us calling each other when we want the physical presence of a human being around—either while doing work or sleeping at night beside each other. Since both of us know why we are meeting and have discussions around it, this enhances our well-being. It allows us to meet our needs of wanting human presence and touch. It allows us to feel less lonely, more complete. We feel energised and more productive the following day, whenever we share the bed or cuddle.

Lately, I have been trying to navigate orgasms. It has been ingrained in me (mainly through porn) that sex is centred around the man's pleasure, that sex without the man orgasming is not sex. Most porn videos have a set routine of some foreplay, an extended blowjob by the woman, different sexual positions, mostly involving peno-vaginal intercourse, ending with the man ejaculating on the woman. However, recently, I haven't orgasmed or felt the need to. I find sex more interesting when I try to focus on the pleasure of the woman I am with, either by trying to understand the ways in which she is responding to my actions through her movements and her breath, or by just following what I am told to do instead of expecting things to play out like a porn sequence. And in doing so, I am able to reflect on what my needs are and thus delineate them from how I have been told sex should be.

Being this way challenges my masculine notions of sex—I have been choosing it consciously, but it has revealed new pleasures and helped me cope with some insecurities most men have, instead of brushing them under the carpet. I really enjoy providing pleasure to the woman I am with. So that means sometimes doing away with the traditional penis-in-vagina thrusting that I've been conditioned to believe is the standard, and focusing more on giving clitoral orgasms with my fingers, hands, knees or thighs. I have realised the importance of being constantly aware of how the person is responding and verbally asking if she would be okay with a particular move, the necessity for taking things slow and providing enough space and time for the woman to be able to respond.

Here's one more thing I've learnt: I do not properly know how to have peno-vaginal intercourse. Most of the time, I do not know how to express this apprehension. Usually, it is the woman who guides me. At times, I am embarrassed that I do not know how to go about it. But I had never discussed this with either the men or women in my life, until I spoke to a male friend a few weeks ago.

For the first time, I had an honest conversation with this friend and shared my apprehensions, fears and doubts. We talked about our first sexual experiences, and discussed the fact that we are really unaware of so many different aspects surrounding sex, such as how to put on a condom, how to navigate consent at different points during sex, how to talk about our likes and dislikes, how to have peno-vaginal intercourse, how to identify the clitoris or the vagina and, most importantly, how to ensure a fulfilling sexual experience for both ourselves and our partners. We lamented the fact that we never received sex education either in our schools or from our parents. My friend explained that he had to surf the Internet to understand how to put on a condom, how to have intercourse, how to please a woman. We even talked about how masturbating for about twenty-five years and then finally having a sexual relationship affects the way in which we have sex. (Certain sexual positions make us come faster—and thus 'last' lesser in bed—because we are used to masturbating in a particular way. At times, we are so used to masturbating that we prefer that over sex since it's the only thing that makes us ejaculate.)

We also touched upon the pressure to 'perform' when it comes to sex. I told him something I had never ever spoken about before—recently, when I was with a woman, I lost my erection as soon as I tried putting on a condom, and again as soon as I tried to put my penis in her vagina. He wondered why it might have happened, speculating that perhaps it was because of stress. And I think that sharing something personal with him opened up room for him to do the same. He told me that he had looked up how to last longer in bed. Apparently, if you first make your partner come, your confidence will increase, and then you can go on to have a longer session of intercourse. He did tell me that there was a phase of about a week when he was coming too soon and that felt shameful. But then he said with a grin that he was able to get his mojo back and last longer in bed after that. At this point, I couldn't help but ask him if he had checked what his partner thought of all of this and if her pleasure actually comes from longer intercourse or if she prefers other aspects of seeking pleasure. He confirmed that they did have a conversation about that, and that she was also very supportive whenever he came too early, reassuring him that it was okay for it to happen, that he shouldn't feel bad. And we found out that while in porn the pleasure is centred around the man, in our relationships we actually both enjoy giving pleasure to our partners in the way they want us to.

I felt relieved to be able to talk about these things with someone. After we went back to our homes, we both texted each other expressing how wonderful the conversation was and how great it was to spend time this way. I also realised that if I don't bring such topics up and make myself vulnerable, I won't ever get to have such conversations with men—since they are unlikely to make that kind of first move!

Right now, these times feel like the heyday of my exploration of and reflection on my needs surrounding care, sex, love and affection. These are also the first few times I am honestly and constructively dealing with my apprehensions and emotions about sex, consent and relationships with myself and with the men and women in my lives. It is a slow process of really trying to understand how not to deal with loneliness—as men, we are conditioned to deal with longing for physical touch, presence, affection and intimacy in a ridiculously traditional masculine manner through tonnes of porn, alcohol, weed, gaming and sports; through conversations with men about everything other than our lives; or through sex that disregards our partner's body or emotions. I've learnt that feminism is about practising goodness, kindness, empathy and affection—both towards oneself and others. These things may not make me very 'manly' by the warped standards I grew up with. But they're making me a better (and, I think, happier) person.

Sudhamshu is a cis-male still exploring the spectrum of sexuality and a waking (never woke) practitioner of feminist ways of being. Professionally, he is a researcher from Bangalore.

Happy Ending

PRAGYA LAL

1

In the time you took to respond to my text
I got a driver's licence
Drove all the way to Nepal from Bangalore
And started a family with a man named Diljeet
Diljeet speaks my love language
Emotional intimacy doesn't spook him
Diljeet speaks my love language
Public opinion doesn't spook him
Diljeet speaks my love language
Even paperwork and government officials don't spook him
Instead,
He guards my heart,
Enjoys my art,
He gets my flowers,
Makes me whiskey sours
I spank his bum
And he makes me cum
Again
Again and
Again

2

In the time you took to respond to my text
I uninstalled all dating apps

And ordered a vibrator online
I started by
Erasing all the trivia about Chelsea F.C., drones and death metal from the depths of my brain
Then went on to
Unlearn the taste of your favourite food, the way you smelt and parted your hair
Unlike you,
My vibrator is
Available
Dependable and
Secure (can you imagine?)
Unlike you,
It doesn't interrupt my sentences
It doesn't pretend to be feminist to get laid
It never tries to explain Reddit to me—very slowly
Unlike you,
It makes me cum
Again
Again and
Again

Pragya Lal writes poems to keep the universe on its toes.

Acknowledgements

The biggest thank you for the existence of this book is to the many agents of ishq who made up Agents of Ishq by sliding into our inboxes with, 'I have a story and I don't want it anywhere but on AOI.' Some stories are in these pages, but many more are on the website. They collectively imagined this universe with us.

Thank you to the Agents of Ishq community who commented, shared, critiqued and built the conversation that surrounds this book.

I have had many editorial colleagues over the years, and thanks go to each of them for the empathy, skill, commitment and productive disagreement they brought to the work. But most of all to Deepika S., with whom in the foundational years, we jumped headfirst into this unexpected work of shaping the stories we received. Together, we slowly evolved a capacious yet rigorous editorial framework. Her steady, affectionate and gentle persistence are very special. In later years, Gitanjali Chandrashekhar, Deepanjana Pal, Ahana Basu and Shweta Dash have all been part of adding to this work.

Thank you to the many AOI colleagues over the last decade. Their impassioned conversations about every piece and each image, their ability to look at the stories with excitement, their honesty and deep involvement have helped to continually expand the boundaries of what is possible and beautiful. Afrah Shafiq, Deepika Sharma and Sonal Giani, who were co-travellers when this baby was born; Debasmita Das, Umang Sabarwal, Olimpika Ojha, Hamsi and Anshumaan Sathe who helped it to walk and talk and walk the talk.

To my agent Jayapriya Vasudevan for her constant enthusiasm, encouragement, indulgence in the face of my overthinking and non-deadline keeping—thank you for that, and the pink drinks. To Karthika VK, for wanting this book, because what a thing it is to be loved. It makes all things possible—thank you.

Thank you to Sameera Iyengar, my friend and colleague, for her steadfastness and her Excel sheet magic, and always thinking about what I need to do work I love and for the sev puri treats.

Thank you to Toral Shah, brilliant, practical, loving, supportive reader and comrade. Our interns Ananya Aulakh Pathak, Fatima Tambawalla, Kanishka Bomb and Harshada Deokar, who read, collated, wrote emails, filled Excel sheets with data and the office with smarts, heart and intriguing tiffins.

Thank you to *The Ladies Finger* and all its founders, for being a pioneer and an inspiration of how we can make vibrant, truthful, intelligent, desi feminist spaces on the Internet, and for sometimes being partners in passion and politics.

Anand Sinha, Vanita Nayak and Pramada Menon—thank you for supporting the project at different times.

My friends Samina Mishra and Hansa Thapliyal have attentively and patiently held my hand through every enterprise, through my every desire and mistake. Without their wisdom and love, this book would have less heart.

All work happens in community and in conversation with the work of others. Many were the conversations (that have fed and watered this project over the years) had with Ruchir Joshi, Anjali Arondekar, Francesca Orsini, Nisha

Susan, Abhijit Dutta, Jugal Mody, Amrita Narayanan, Rahul Srivastava, Aneela Zeb Babar and Amrita Dutta. Their belief, their brightness and their timepass jokes shone like stars over different parts of my journey with Agents of Ishq.

Thank you to the friends who were always there with a helping hand, advice and affection—Devdutt Pattanaik, Amruta Patil and Bishakha Datta.

Last but not the least, thank you to my mum and dad, in their different ways, for making me an Unlimited Girl and for passing on to me the appetite for pleasure and friendship and tight hugs. That has been the masala with which I have cooked this life, and this book. Thank you.